THE
Archive Photographs
SERIES

PENTYRCH, CREIGIAU
AND GWAELOD Y GARTH

Mari Lwyd with Twm Davies (Caerwal) and his son Trefor.

THE Archive Photographs SERIES
PENTYRCH, CREIGIAU
AND GWAELOD Y GARTH

Compiled by
Pentyrch and District Local History Society

CHALFORD

First published 1997
Copyright © Pentyrch and District Local History Society, 1997

The Chalford Publishing Company
St Mary's Mill, Chalford,
Stroud, Gloucestershire, GL6 8NX

ISBN 0 7524 0776 7

Typesetting and origination by
The Chalford Publishing Company
Printed in Great Britain by
Redwood Books, Trowbridge

Cover picture:
The family of the local dyn dŵr *(waterman) Enoc Dafydd and his wife Mariah*
gathered to celebrate the couple's golden wedding anniversary, 1900.

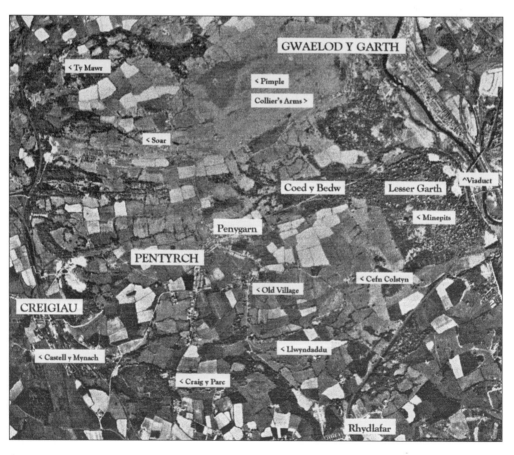

Contents

Part of the 'Old Village' of Pentyrch in 1894 said to be pictured on the wedding day of the vicar's daughter. The church stands where St Catwg formed a Christian cell near a 'magic' spring in the sixth century. The newly built vicarage is on the right and in the centre the Rock and Castle pub is doing fine trade. Centre right is Castle House on the fortified site from which the old tavern took its name; the row of white houses attached to it was converted the following year into the English Mission Hall. The thatched cottages centre left were pulled down in the 1920s and Tŷ Gwellt behind the church on the extreme left remained until the late 1950s. In the upper village, Caerwal Terrace (later Field Row) and Horeb Calvinistic Methodist chapel can be seen.

One warm afternoon in summertime during the 1890s Mrs Thomas was behind the bar of the Rock and Castle when she heard footsteps on the flagstoned floor and saw the moving shadow of a person coming in through the open doorway. 'It's you Ned, isn't it?' she asked of the diminutive figure, now at the bar. Ned the dwarf nodded and she went on:
'Haven't you heard Ned? You were buried last month in the churchyard across the road. Drowned it is you were. In the Taff it was.'

'Yes' said Ned. 'I've only nipped out for a quick drink. I'll be going back straight away.'

Introduction

By Don Llewellyn, Chairman of Pentyrch and District Local History Society.

The old and proud parish of Pentyrch, which includes the villages of Creigiau and Gwaelod y Garth, has now been drawn into the ever-growing city of Cardiff. Ultimately, urban sprawl might destroy these communities, but this collection of photographs will help to record their essential character.

Ancient peoples lived, worked, fought and worshipped on our hillsides; on every flank of the parish, there are sites of great antiquity. The northern skyline is dominated by the Garth Mountain where Bronze Age burial mounds stand as graphic reminders of prehistory. Stone Age implements have been found in a cave of the Lesser Garth on the parish's eastern edge, while a cromlech has stood at Caerarfau on the western boundary for more than five thousand years. Completing the prehistoric picture is the site of an Iron Age fortified homestead at Llwyndaddu on the southern approaches to Pentyrch. It is known that Romans came and fulfilled their needs from the rich and easily accessible mineral deposits in the area. During the Age of Saints which followed, Catwg Ddoeth (Cadoc the Wise) left his mark by forming his bond village around a 'magic' well known since as Ffynnon Catwg. We still hear echoes of the sixth century when we speak of Nant Gwladus, the stream which runs from the well through the old village, for it carries the name of Catwg's mother. In the Middle Ages, despite numerous incursions by Saxons and Normans, Pentyrch survived with its allegiance to the Welsh lords unshaken.

Until the last century, the whole of the area was known as Pentyrch. Creigiau, to the west, did not exist before 1896 when the new railway station on the Barry line took its name from a Pentyrch farm known as Criga. Previously, the cluster of houses which stood nearby had been called Castle Hamlet, after Castell y Mynach, a local gentry house. At the eastern end of the parish, Gwaelod y Garth, formerly known as 'Lower Pentyrch' acquired its separate identity much earlier, coming into being as a result of intense industrial activity in that quarter. Iron production, which had begun seriously in Elizabethan times, flourished again in the eighteenth and nineteenth centuries when the main works was situated at what is now called Garth Newydd. High quality steam coal was obtained from several drift mines. The ravages of mineral extraction left few scars and the essential rural character of the parish was never lost. Thatched cottages and sturdy stone-built farmhouses gave the area a feeling of timelessness, until they, like many other treasures of the past, fell victim to what we call progress.

Since it was formed four years ago, the Pentyrch and District Local History Society has gathered a huge amount of interesting information about the past. Such is the enthusiasm of our membership, which includes both older inhabitants and new residents, that it has been possible to stage three very successful exhibitions in this time. Besides learning from our large collection of documents, we draw heavily upon the very strong local oral tradition. Tape recordings made with elderly people (mostly in Welsh) in the mid-1960s have been invaluable; besides containing sparkling gems of wisdom and wit, the recordings give us a clear idea of the way people felt and behaved a century ago. There is, however, little that can be compared with the immediacy and permanence of a photograph in conveying and recording an historical event. The images which grace these pages depict long gone lifestyles and such diverse personalities as Horatio Thomas, vicar of the parish for forty-seven years, 'Twm Crydd' the humble poacher, Charles Prichard the polymath, R.G. Berry the dramatist, and Twm Lee the pugilist who thrice beat the mighty 'Tiger' Smith. Farmers, coal miners, quarrymen and schoolmasters share this parish picture story with rugby footballers, the hunting fraternity and children at school and at play.

It should be noted that Welsh was the first language of the majority of native inhabitants for much of the period covered by this book. Uniquely, in this anglicised corner of Wales, the Pentyrch Parish Council kept its minutes in both English and Welsh right up to the time of the local authority changes of the 1970s. The old parish area, administered by Pentyrch Community Council, is now a suburb of Cardiff. The move has meant that the capital has gained not only a mountain for the first time but also three villages determined to retain their identities.

According to Professor G.J. Williams, the eminent historian who lived at Gwaelod y Garth, the people of Pentyrch parish were bonded by their common awareness of an ancient attachment to the area. In the oral tradition, a number of families claimed descent from Llewelyn ap Cynwrig, a medieval lord of the manors of Radyr and Pentyrch. Such a strong sense of belonging mystified outsiders who reacted by keeping Pentyrch parishioners at a safe distance. Whenever 'trouble' arose at fairs and markets in the surrounding villages, the sayings *Bit ryddoch chwi wŷr Pentyrch* and *Rhwng gwŷr Pentyrch a'i gilydd* would be heard suggesting that Pentyrch people were better left alone! As we live in more enlightened times may we hope that our attempts to recapture a little of the past of these special villages will be welcomed by all.

Upper Pentyrch – Penygarn, in 1957 when most of the old terraced houses were being pulled down. The open fields were to give way to modern housing estates under a strictly controlled 'Village Development Plan'.

One

Worship

In the sixth century a cell was established by the wise monk Catwg at a tranquil spot in a small valley recess, where the Lord has been fervently praised ever since. The original bond villagers, converted by Catwg would come to this sacred place for their devotions. For many generations, these British Christians would have to continue resisting pressure from the pagan Saxons and Danes who, from time to time, overran the lower Vale. From the Norman period onward the church at Pentyrch, which had belonged to the monks of Llancarfan, came under the control of the bishops of the diocese of Llandaff. The present structure, built in 1857/58, replaced what is thought to have been a church consisting of a simple nave and chancel, with bell cot and priest's door.

There was a strong movement of Dissenters in Pentyrch and the Nonconformists gained an early hold. It is known that the great Howel Harris preached at Pentyrch ten times. From the 1740s Methodists met regularly and, with the Baptist and Congregationalist causes growing rapidly, there were many defections from the established church. Several sites in the parish are said to have been meeting houses for breakaway sects, among them Brista Fach and Y Soar. It is recorded that barns were used for very early clandestine, but later licensed, meetings of Baptists. The Wesleyans had a meeting house in Temperance Road in the 1880s and there were also a few devotees of the Unitarian persuasion in the villages.

By the 1830s, Horeb (Calvinistic Methodist, now Presbyterian Church of Wales) and Penuel (Baptist) stood on the sites they still occupy today, although the latter is no longer a house of worship. Bronllwyn (Congregationalist) followed in 1858 as an off-shoot from Taihirion which had served the community well for many generations. At Gwaelod y Garth, Bethlehem (Independent) chapel began in 1830 as both a religious and educational centre. In later years Salem (Baptist) also played its part in the busy religious and cultural life of Gwaelod y Garth. Today, Bethlehem continues but Salem is a private residence.

In 1895, Mr. J.W.C. Schroeter, a Norwegian Consul, who had business interests connected with the importation of Scandinavian timber, financed the conversion of four cottages adjoining Castle House into an English Mission Hall. This was to provide the small but growing number of English-only speakers with religious services they could understand.

During the 'Revival' of 1904, huge crowds turned out to hear Evan Roberts preach at open-air meetings on Y Forlan fields and many conversions took place at early morning gatherings on the Garth.

Remarkably, despite the strength of the Christian faith many locals held onto their belief in the supernatural. The historian Edgar L. Chappell said that Pentyrch residents had been great believers in bendith y mamau (fairies) and lived in fear of traditional ghosts like the ladi wen (white lady) and the ceffyl dŵr (water horse). Lording it over all these apparitions was y brenin llwyd (king of the mist) who was said to reside in the old iron-ore mine of the Lesser Garth. Even in the present century there have been alleged sightings of the ladi wen and phantom funerals. Superstitions are not so prevalent now.

St Catwg's Church in Wales is still strong today and the Mission has its faithful flock. Horeb opens its doors but is in dire need of a revival. Bronllwyn has been replaced by the village hall. The decline of the chapels is one of the more telling examples of severe change to have taken place in living memory. Not so long ago if one stood on the groeslon (High Corner crossroads) on a Sunday evening, hymns of praise in four-part harmony could be heard coming from several different directions.

St Catwg's church pictured in 1899. It was rebuilt in 1857, during the long incumbency of Horatio James Thomas, by John Prichard, the diocesan architect, and his partner John Seddon. In their preferred late-thirteenth century Gothic style, this small church, built at a cost of less than £1,500, is particularly beautiful, with its soaring effect and graceful spire.

Revd Horatio James Thomas, vicar of Pentyrch from 1834 to 1880, was perpetual curate of Llantwit Vardre for over fifty years. He was an evangelical churchman, who defied the thirteenth-century architecture of his new church by placing the pulpit in front of the altar and using the building as a protestant 'preaching box'. He was a Welshman of local stock whose services were exclusively in the Welsh language throughout his incumbency; yet, he could not stem the rise of Nonconformity in his parishes. Hannah, his wife, was a local farmer's daughter with deep roots in the parish. Her brother Daniel Williams, tenant of Llwyndaddu, was a keen huntsman and a noted breeder of black and tan Welsh foxhounds.

Equine and Canine, c. 1850. The horse is said to have belonged to Revd Horatio James Thomas. It is therefore assumed that the building on the far left is St Catwg's. If so, then the oil painting is the only existing evidence of what the church looked like before being completely rebuilt in 1857.

St Peter's Mission (the 'Tin Church') was built in 1907 to serve the people of Gwaelod y Garth who, due to the 'extraordinary elevations and the poor state of the roads' were unable to attend the parish church of St Catwg. Sited on the Gwaelod road below Tynewydd it had a relatively short life, closing in 1938.

Pentyrch, 1936. The ancient nucleus of the parish is still known affectionately as 'The Old Village'. Nearly fifteen hundred years ago Catwg (Cadoc the Wise) trod his way to this spot, as did the sandalled monks who followed in the footsteps of that great and good man. For centuries (until the 1940s) water from the 'magic' spring which brought the saintly sage to Pentyrch, emerged from a spout in a wall at the churchyard perimeter. This was the only water supply for the community and the spring marked the traditional meeting place for gossip.

Tŷ Rhawn and Bro Nant, 1921. The lower part of the 'Old Village' has ancient associations. The little stream which runs down this valley is called Nant Gwladus after the mother of Catwg. The sites of an Iron Age fort but a stone's throw away and of a castle just up the hill, give this part of the hamlet an air of great antiquity. A century ago, customers of the Bute Arms, now Bro Nant, would have had plenty to talk about.

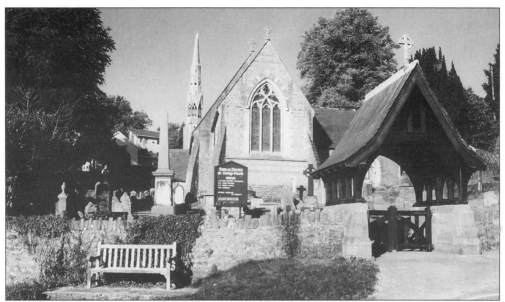

A Christian foundation has existed here since about 550 AD. Surviving ancient records include Papal Bulls of 1128 and 1129 and a document of 1147 records a grant made to the 'brethren of Pendar' (Margam Abbey) witnessed by 'Eniauun, Presbyter de Pentirech'. The church has changed little since being rebuilt in 1857, except for the beautiful lych-gate designed and donated in 1944 by Mr Thomas Henry Sparks, admired architect, churchwarden and devoted servant of St Catwg's.

Choir of St Catwg's church, Pentyrch, 1958. The vicar Revd L.C. Gruffydd Jones is on the left and on the right is the curate Hugh Grenville Godden. Back row: Adrian and Ralph Perrett, Gladys Evans, Cyril Perrett, D. Godden. Middle row: Graham Chamberlain, Huw Davies, Vivian Llewellyn, Gerald Langdon, Tom Middleton, John Davies (organist). Front: Richard Grenville Godden, John Langdon, John and Glenys Morris.

Penuel, Pentyrch, 1938. A hundred years earlier, on 28 April 1838, with others, John Thomas of Tŷ Du, in Capel Llanilltern, obtained a licence for their new Baptist chapel. It was built on Y Dwrlyn, then part of Cefn Colstyn. It retains a religious link as the workshop of an organ builder.

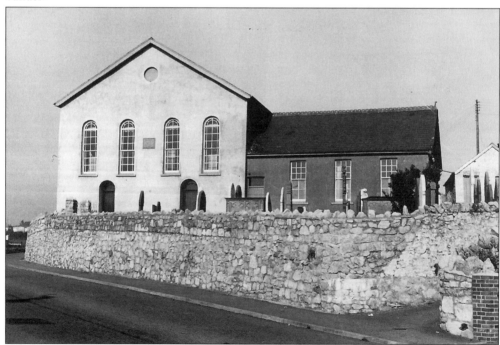

Horeb, Capel y Methodistiaid Calfinaidd. Founded in 1740 as a Methodist Society at Brista Fach, the first structure on the later site was built by Evan Williams of Baily Coch in the 1830s. His younger brother Job Williams of Y Gocyd rebuilt the chapel in 1862. It now serves the Presbyterian Church of Wales.

Taihirion, 1930. This chapel dating from 1829, played a prominent part in the history of Glamorgan Congregationalism, founding four neighbourhood churches, including Bronllwyn in Pentyrch. Revd John Taihirion Davies, later of Tabernacl, Efail Isaf, was instrumental in this move. Taihirion was established about 1761 on land given by the Williams family of Parc y Justice. Their successor, Mr Samuel Price, a Presbyterian, left them £200 on his death in 1777. A notable member was 'Jim yr Enjin' a converted pugilist. In 1918 the congregation affiliated to the English-speaking Association. Now a ruin, the land has reverted to Tŷ Du farm.

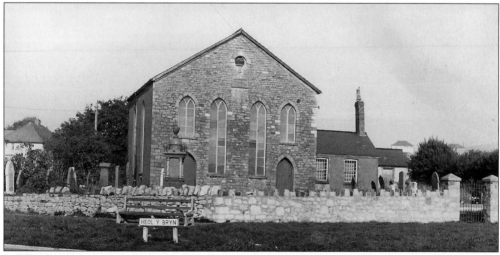

Bronllwyn, Capel yr Annibynwyr (Congregationalist chapel), in 1965, five years before it was demolished. Founded from Taihirion in 1858 by Revd John Taihirion Davies, it was built by the redoubtable Thomas Williams, three of whose family were among the original twelve members. The services at this meeting house for local 'Independents' were entirely in Welsh and well attended until the numbers dwindled in the 1960s. In 1970 it was pulled down and Pentyrch Village Hall now stands on the site.

A scene at the church gate, *c.* 1895. This unidentified picture is not a funeral for they chose a white horse; also the dress and headgear in evidence are bright and informal. It might be a summer holy festival, possibly Whitsuntide. It could well be a christening for at least one baby can be seen in the arms of a lady near the door. It is thought likely to be a wedding and as most of the 'guests' appear to be making their way towards the church, it would be too early for the gate to be tied up in the manner of the local custom. After the ceremony, the bride and groom would not be allowed through the gate until the best man had thrown a handful of pennies to a throng of youngsters sure to be waiting outside. At this time, the quaint custom of firing a cannon was followed at weddings to enliven the proceedings. A rectangular iron block with cylindrical holes, made in the 1850s at Pentyrch Works, was used until 1900 when the practice was discontinued after an accident. A guest prematurely approached the block, which had been charged in the usual way with gunpowder, to inspect a suspected misfire. His leg was blown over the church roof.

The Mission, Pentyrch, 1960. Four cottages attached to Castle House were converted in 1895 into the 'English Mission Hall' largely due to the efforts of Mr J.W.C. Schroeter, a consul and Norwegian timber importer, who lived at Greenhurst and was a partner of Frederick De Courcy Hamilton. At that time, in all the houses of worship including the parish church, all the services were conducted in Welsh only. The new Mission Hall was to provide the only English language services for the growing number of immigrants to the area.

Ysgol Sul (Sunday school), Horeb, Pentyrch, 1936. At the back: Gwyneth Evans, Ruth Llewellyn, Katie Lewis. Standing: Sid Llewellyn, Joey Llewellyn, Idwal Stevens, Howard Lewis, Eirlys Thomas, Betty Edwards. Seated: Connie Gould, Val Regan, Megan Williams, Betty Willicombe, Barbara Gould, Edith Edwards, Doris Willicombe. In front: Billy Jones, Joan Williams, Gwyn Williams, Donald Ham.

The barn at Cefn Colstyn, Pentyrch, 1900. Buildings like these, dating from about 1790-1820, were sometimes licensed to hold religious meetings. In 1832 local Baptists were permitted to hold services in 'a barn formerly occupied by Evan Morgan of Cefn Colstyn'. It could have been this one, or as is more likely, a barn which stood on the site where Penuel chapel was built.

Group outing c. 1900, probably Mission Hall members on a walk to the Garth. The group certainly includes the Mission's founder Mr J.W.C. Schroeter in the centre. At the back are some of the staff of Pentyrch school including Mr Charles Graham Hughes.

Two

Work

For centuries the inhabitants of Pentyrch were able to find work locally; today they generally commute to employment outside the parish. In 1801, three quarters of the population was classed as 'involved in agriculture'. The farmers of Graig Gwilym, Tyncoed, Blaen Bielli and Cwm Llwydrew, also mined coal and gave employment to men who left the land marked with hundreds of depressions from the bell pits sunk to extract coal from shallow deposits. The iron works which had restarted in the 1740s employed ironstone miners, furnace and forge workers. Within thirty years the population tripled as a result of the Europe-wide population explosion following the end of the Napoleonic wars and the influx of workers attracted to the surging coal and iron industries. Specialist engineers came from the declining industrial centres such as Ironbridge and farm workers came from Somerset and Berkshire to replace local agricultural labourers who were transferring to hazardous but better-paid mining jobs.

What we today call the extractive industry was based on the rich mineral resources in the parish, sitting as it does astride the southern outcrop of the South Wales coalfield. The northern half of the parish – the village of Gwaelod y Garth, the Garth mountain and the lower adjacent Graig Gwilym – is grey sandstone with outcrops of coal seams on the southern faces and many seams of better quality steam coal at the lowest levels. South of a line drawn from Garth Newydd through Penygarn and to the Caesar's Arms the rocks are mainly Carboniferous limestone, containing massive iron-ore bodies in the Lesser Garth with the higher magnesium-containing Dolomitic variety occurring in the east. Between the two is a mixed zone containing aggregates and clay or shale beds, extensively mined for the underlying coal in the past.

Sandstone quarries on the Garth and lime kilns to the south provided building materials and lime for agriculture. Increased demand for iron products was satisfied in the 1840s and 50s with new blast furnaces, puddling and refining plant and an enlarged iron mine on the Lesser Garth, firstly with new lifting gear then a tunnel, providing a shorter exit route for spoil and sorted ore for the furnace. Coke for the furnaces came from ovens fed with Bedw mine and Lan colliery coal. A claypit on the Gwaelod y Garth road provided the material for coke oven, furnace lining and structural bricks and the nearby Pentyrch Brickworks survived the cessation of the iron industry there. The collapse of the iron works around 1880 resulted from non-competitive operating costs, a lack of investment to produce the 'mild steel' increasingly demanded for construction and transport and finally the collapse of the bank financing the iron works. Coal extraction costs could not compete with deep pit operations in the valleys and the coal levels successively closed.

Although the opening of Creigiau quarry in the 1870s had provided work for some, this was a period of great hardship. Increasingly, miners travelled daily to the Cynon and Rhondda valley mines, others travelled to Cardiff. The South Cambria colliery opened at Tyncoed in 1895 providing mining employment, but closed in 1915 due to costs and declining demand for its coal. By 1930 the extractive industry had been reduced to limestone quarrying at Creigiau, the Steetley Dolomite plant producing feedstock for the steel industry, and small stone quarries supplying construction projects.

Farming activity has continued, with adjustments in its nature to suit the prevailing demand and with a general decline in the numbers of people involved. The bleak prospects of the post-First World War years continued through the 1920s to the mid-1930s when the opening of Trefforest Trading Estate offered some increased job opportunities. Rumours of war and the Second World War itself in fact restored full employment to the area but we now see few local opportunities, apart from those serving the parish itself: retailers, those involved in education, worship and the public service industries. Today the old parish is an attractive living base for those who commute, especially to the city of Cardiff for employment.

The Minepits. Iron ore deposits in the limestone core of the Lesser Garth have been extracted for the production of iron, possibly since Roman times or earlier. Up to the mid-1840s the ore was drawn up from open pits by winches or 'whims', manual or horse-operated lifting drums. Horse or donkey trains then transported the ore in panniers to the blast furnaces. About 1847 lifting gear and a steam engine were installed at the top to increase the rate of ore removal. Within ten years this was inadequate for the quantity required and a horizontal adit was constructed from the pit base to allow removal of the ore nearer to the old Pentyrch road, and tramway conveyance to the furnace. Subsequently, mining continued for some two hundred feet or so below this level, and when mining ceased about 1879 the vast chambers left, filled with water to leave awesome pools. The picture shows light streaming in from the surface, passages leading off from the main road into the pits, and a deep water-filled chasm. Engineer John Cazel, born in Wolverhampton, came to operate the steam engine in 1847 via Llwydcoed, near Aberdare, then Maesmawr colliery. About a century later, in the Second World War, his great-grandson climbed the fence guarding the pit, then used as a Ministry of Supply munitions dump, and marvelled at the small railway down below moving yellow ammunition containers to storage points. A decade later, now in the empty pit with calcite crystals sparkling in the torchlight, the enormous pools were seen for the first time by the same great-grandson.

An elevated view of the old Pentyrch furnace. This represents the second stage of the manufacture of iron in Pentyrch, which commenced in the 1740s and finally closed about 1879 bringing great poverty to the area. The first Pentyrch ironworks commenced about 1565 and closed about 1620. It specialised in the 'manufacture of the finest ordnance in the country' and it is believed that cannon manufactured at this site were used in the defeat of the Spanish Armada in 1588. However, as a result of the illegal export of cannon to 'enemies of the realm', the destruction of the furnace was ordered in 1620.

The remains of the coke ovens on the site of the Pentyrch furnace. These ovens were used to convert the locally mined coal into coke for the manufacture of iron; the furnace had previously been fired by charcoal, readily obtained from the surrounding woodland. At the height of production at the plant, there were almost a hundred of these ovens in use.

View from the viaduct. The congested communications can clearly be seen as the Taff Gorge is approached, together with acres of industrial dereliction and waste products resulting from iron manufacture. The extent of the community living on the side of the Garth can also be appreciated – the 1881 census indicated that almost forty families lived there.

The derelict Pentyrch furnace, much of which is already being reclaimed by nature, pictured about 1905. The quarry on the right, Cwarre Glas, provided limestone necessary for the production of iron. Iron ore was obtained from the Lesser Garth and originally taken to the furnace by donkey, but was later, together with the coal from Coed y Bedw, conveyed to Cwarre Glas and lowered down an incline by a balance system to the furnace below.

Construction of the Walnut Tree viaduct. The viaduct was built for the Barry Docks and Railway Company and designed to speed the transport of coal, mined particularly in the Monmouthshire valleys, to the new docks at Barry. Designed by Sir James W. Szlumper, its construction began in 1898.

The Walnut Tree viaduct was finally dismantled during 1968 and '69. Despite the use of substantial lifting gear, the demolition was attended by a few mishaps, one involving the fall of a crane from the top of one of the piers.

Creigiau pottery was started by Mr Reginald Southcliffe soon after the end of the Second World War and continued until the 1970s. Situated on the Llantwit Road beyond the Caesar's Arms, the pottery was just outside the parish boundary. Nevertheless, it helped put Creigiau on the map, receiving a large number of visitors and its products, including prized copper lustre items, were sent to many parts of the world.

The 'Forgie Line' runs alongside the feeder towards the viaduct. This line was built in 1815 to transport the castings and forgings from the Pentyrch Ironworks to the tinplate works at Melingriffith. Later (about 1848), it was connected into the Taff Vale railway at Ynys Gau. The rolling stock was run by steam engines – the 'Verdun' being replaced in 1936 by the 'Princess May'.

A railway maintenance crew takes a breather to pose for this photograph – believed to be on the 'Forgie Line' at Salem sidings. The crew includes William Davies and James Welsby. As well as being hand-propelled, the truck could be lifted off the single-track line to allow other railway vehicles to pass. The youngsters of the village also had a lot of fun with this truck after the workmen had gone home!

The Walnut Tree viaduct in the early 1920s with the buildings of the Pentyrch Forge in the foreground. The houses alongside the main road can be seen clearly. The stack, built in 1866, was constructed from bricks manufactured at the Pentyrch brickworks. The 'eagle' on the south side of the stack had two 'shining eyes' which resulted from the insertion of two bottles of ale, purchased from the Lewis's Arms in Tongwynlais.

A view of the Garth with the weir and the Taff's Well mineral spring in the foreground. The weir was constructed in 1790 to provide a source of water for the Pentyrch forge. The water was carried by a feeder to the forge, where it was used to power machinery and was then returned to the river above Morganstown. When the weir was removed in the late 1960s as a flood prevention measure, it was found that the 'greenheart' ridge timbers were in pristine condition.

These old cottages were built to house Pentyrch Furnace workers and were known variously as 'Orles Row', 'Square Row', and 'New Level Houses'. Because of the low-lying ground and the proximity of both the river and the feeder, they were often flooded. Also in the picture is the Mission Hall, associated with the Tin Church on the Gwaelod road. Following demolition of the cottages in the 1940s, the site became a refuse dump, but has since been reclaimed and is currently home to Taff's Well RFC.

William Rees of Willowford at work at the site of one of the many coal levels in Coed Rhiw Ceiliog. It is thought that the steam boiler in the picture provided power for the raising and lowering of coal drams up and down an incline, transporting the coal from the level to the ironworks in the valley below.

The Pentyrch brickworks occupied the site which now comprises the junction of Heol Berry and Heol y Nant. It began by using waste fireclay from the Lan colliery to make bricks which were used for the later buildings of Pentyrch Forge, the furnace and of the Lan colliery. However the business developed independently of the iron manufacturing, and survived long after the closure of that operation. The house shown was built as an office, but is now a domestic residence.

View from Cwarre Glas c. 1906, with the buildings of the Lan colliery shown clearly in the centre of the photograph. This colliery worked the Brass and Forked seams about 700 yards into the hillside, and was the scene of a disaster in 1875 when an explosion resulted in the death of twelve men and boys. The bricked-up entrance can still be seen. Below the Lan is the Pentyrch brickworks which derived its raw material from the claypit in Maesgwyn field, on the left of the picture.

Creigiau quarry *c*. 1885. Quarrying began here in the 1870s. Stone was taken for the building of Cardiff docks and road developments. Later, the quarry helped to meet the demand for limestone required by the steel-making industry and provided steady employment for a number of Pentyrch workers.

Creigiau quarry workers, 1933. Among the group are Aubrey Betty, Tom, Billy and Llewellyn Davies (Caerwal), Tommy Rees, Ollie Richards, Dai and Emrys Thomas (Mari), Fred Griffiths and Idris Stephens. Quarry manager Jack Jones is seated in the middle of the front row.

Completing the landscaping of the gardens at Craig y Parc, Pentyrch, 1926. In the centre with the wheelbarrow is Mr Charles John, who had retired as a coal trimmer at Barry, and like many other local men was helping to make the gardens amongst the best in Glamorgan. Tom Edmunds on the left and Noah Lewis, second right, are also of old Pentyrch stock.

Thomas Jenkins ('Twm Crydd') helping to construct the entrance to one of the three drifts at the South Cambria mine in Tyncoed, Pentyrch, at the commencement of the operation of the Cambrian Collieries Syndicate in 1895.

Tyncoed, 1905. Three drift mines, providing steam coal, were operated by the Cambrian Collieries Syndicate here from 1895 until 1915. While nature has restored the area to its former sylvan glory, two of the entrances can still be seen.

Mishap at Tyncoed. Extensive use was made of horses both beneath and above ground at the colliery. Inevitably there was the occasional problem such as this derailment involving a few drams. From the size of carriages and horses these would have been for surface movements only.

The kilns at Steetley Dolomite Quarry and Works, 1938. The extraction and processing of first-grade dolomite, required by the steel-making industry, gave employment to many from Pentyrch, Gwaelod y Garth and Taff's Well. It had been a large scale operation since 1925 when the big Midlands firm took over the small burnt lime unit run by a Captain Burns.

The kiln workers have just finished their break and are ready for another afternoon in the heat and dust. In the middle of the front row is Dai Griffiths whose jokes shortened many a working day. With hands on hips at the ready is Rhys Lewis.

Whereas boat ferries were used elsewhere, prior to the opening of the lower footbridge to Taff's Well, the river at this point was crossed by means of stepping stones. The low level of water is a result of the take-out of water for the Pentyrch Forge at the weir higher up. The huge banks of ironworks slag were removed for the construction of both Roath and Barry Docks.

Again, the unpredictability of the river is illustrated by the depth of floodwater against the new footbridge, emphasising the effectiveness of the river as a parish boundary.

Y Gwcw (The Cuckoo level), 1975. This hillside, in sight of the 'peak', was an inferno of activity when Malkin visited the area about one hundred and fifty years earlier. The turntable, originally turned by two horses, and rotating a horizontal shaft connected to a winch, is all that remains of the gear which hauled coal and waste up from the coal level here. Interestingly, Pentyrch people were known as 'cuckoos' to outsiders.

Embedded in a garden wall at Craig y Parc is this iron firegrate dated 1743. It was made at Pentyrch Ironworks and used at the Portobello Inn, Taff's Well for 170 years.

Three

Leisure

With priority given to the task of earning a living, leisure time was as precious in Pentyrch parish as it was elsewhere. Those who scratched a livelihood from the land had little time to spare and many coal miners saw natural light only on Sundays. Nevertheless, old customs were enthusiastically followed. According to the oral tradition the parishioners of Pentyrch were keenly involved in the centuries-old inter-village competition known as cnapan. This was a forerunner of football in which the possession of a pig's dried and inflated bladder was contested over many hours and miles with some participants on horseback and others on foot.

The main regular country activity, drawing support from all sections of society was fox-hunting. It is recorded in the school punishment book that the main cause of truancy in the early years of this century was 'following the hounds'. Hunting reached its peak of popularity during the inter-war years when the huntsmen were Jack Evans and Ianto Phillips. Horses have always been prominent features in the life of the parish with the Pentyrch point-to-point races attracting thousands to the village.

Inevitably, as in every country domain, poaching of game has been a way of life. Since the time of George Mathew's deer park and hunting lodge at Craig y Parc men have sought ways of improving their pantry stock and many gifted poachers have left their mark on local history. In sessions of legitimate culling like pheasant shoots, local children were happy to be engaged as beaters.

Septuagenarians, recorded in the 1960s, tell us of their grandparents' favourite games; we learn that bando and quoits were popular in the 1850s as well as bomparino ('strong horses, weak donkeys') a pastime which remained popular in Pentyrch and Gwaelod y Garth until just a few years ago. Conventional modern sports gradually won people over from the traditional pursuits and rugby in particular became an essential part of the fabric of local society. Other sports have been keenly followed too, including soccer and boxing. Tennis thrived long in Pentyrch and Creigiau. Cricket, strong in Pentyrch village between the wars, had an even bigger following in Gwaelod y Garth. Creigiau golf club opened with a nine-hole course in 1921.

People expressed themselves musically through the strong local choral tradition. The John Thomas mixed choirs of Pentyrch, the Garth Gleemen conducted by Will George and the concert parties which graced the stage of Creigiau church hall gave the whole parish a good name for fine singing. During the Second World War Horeb chapel was the venue for community singing evenings which were packed out; these were often attended by soldiers from the US military hospital at Rhydlafar.

The villages had versifiers too, some producing simple doggerel and others whose work reached heights of sublime beauty. These could be found at the Kings, the Rock or the Colliers weaving wondrous words with that gift of spontaneity which characterised the beirdd gwlad (country poets). On summer evenings they would gather at the bench called 'The Bardic' (Y Fainc Farddol) in Cefn Bychan. At Christmas and New Year, the Mari Lwyd was taken on her excursions to the three villages. The party engaged householders and publicans in intense poetic exchanges which always ended up with much celebration involving food and drink.

Before the Women's Institute became the main organisation for the ladies of Pentyrch and Gwaelod y Garth, another group was very active indeed. The Women's Whist Guild combined its weekly card playing with a series of energetic fund-raising campaigns for a variety of charities.

Organised events such as drama productions, eisteddfodau, fêtes, carnivals, gymkhanas and flower shows have been held over the years in the three villages, also there were impromptu rural activities such as harvesting the ample fruits of the hedgerows. The formal parks which exist in a town are not necessary here, for this parish is itself a large and splendid garden. Hiking and rambling have increased locally in recent years as new residents have become aware of the rural beauty around them.

A joint meeting of Tredegar and Pentyrch Hounds, 1914. The Lewis Arms (Y Twyn) was a favourite location for the gathering of horses and hounds.

'Jac yr Heliwr' (Jack the Huntsman), Pentyrch, 1929. Jack Evans was to retire in 1930, handing over to Evan (Ianto) Phillips who had been his whipper-in. Thirty-six brace of fox were taken in the 1929 season! Jack was back in the huntsman's saddle a few years later. Here he is seen being handed 'the stirrup cup' by Johnny Davies who became his son-in-law.

Pentyrch Rugby Football Club, 1912. Thrown out of the Cardiff and District Union the previous season, they promptly won the Pontypridd and District League and Knockout Competition. Back row: W. Morgan, T. Llewellyn, T. Howells, F. Savage, C. Rees. Third row: J. Llewellyn, I. Jones, G. Prichard, T. David, O. Richards, O. Evans, M. Evans, R. Evans, D. Evans, J. Lloyd. Seated: F. Llewellyn, P. Evans, E. Thomas, T. Buffet (captain), E. Watkins, T. Miles, D. Llewellyn, E. Llewellyn (treasurer). In front: D. Jenkins, I. Llewellyn, E. Jenkins, W.G. Thomas. As 'Ned Cwmllwytro' sang at the time: 'The good old Cardiff District at a verdict did arrive… expelled us for a season but the boys are still alive! To beat the Pentyrch boys, to beat the Pentyrch boys, you must be very clever to beat the Pentyrch boys!'

Pentyrch rugby footballers, 1898.
Back: Idris Jones, Dai John. Front:
Charlie Jenkins, Tom Miles.

Rugby on Clawdd Siôn, 1949. From 1906 until moving to Y Dwrlyn in 1952, Pentyrch RFC played on this field where the Troed y Garth estate now stands. Here Derek Murphy kicks a conversion. The 'ball holder' lying down is Idwal Stephens.

Pentyrch RFC at Cardiff Arms Park, 1952 (Mallett Cup winners for the third time in succession). This team was notable for having three Williams brothers of Craig Gwilym farm in the pack, the three tallest in the back row of the photograph: Glyndwr, Illtyd and Glanffrwd; there would have been four except that eldest brother Maelgwyn had left the club to play for Pontypridd.

Pentyrch soccer team, 1935. Back row: Reg Gibbs, Reg Pattimore, Roy Gardner, Mervyn Jones, Marcus Phillips. Second row: R. Powell, Edgar Davies, Aubrey Gibbs, Cyril Anthony, Bill George, Roy Wood. Front row: Stan Castle, Glyn Evans, Rutter Thomas (president), Tom Llewellyn (captain), Bill Baines (patron), Ken Davies, Tudor Prichard.

Y Soar, 1938. Billy Morse, on the left, became a professional boxer whose career was brought to an end by the advent of the Second World War. His brother Cecil, on the right, also an able fighter, was a regular player with Pentyrch rugby team. The brothers are seen with David Jones and, second from right, Trefor Llewellyn who was coaching Billy in preparation for a forthcoming match in Bristol.

Pentyrch Tennis Club, 1937. The pavilion, adjacent to the school, was erected in 1921 after a campaign led by the curate, Revd Lundy Richards. Two grass courts and a bowling green were available to the club's seventy members in its best years. The pavilion was used for different purposes during the war, but the courts fell into disrepair. The courts were revived in the post-war years but the club failed to re-establish itself fully. Private dwellings were built on the ground in 1960.

The completed Athletic Club building which served as the HQ of Pentyrch RFC from 1955 until the palatial new premises were opened in 1977. At the rear can be seen the 'tin shed' which from 1965 was the licensed social club described affectionately by a WRU representative as 'the only clubhouse in Wales where you had to wipe your feet to come out!'

The official opening of the Garth cricket pavilion in 1935. Most of the players were from Gwaelod y Garth and the surrounding area. The cricket field, known as the Ynys, was originally marshland, but was reclaimed by the manhandling of hundreds of tons of colliery waste from nearby tips. This was carried out by men and boys alike, to create an attractive playing field which became the centrepiece of village life on warm summer Saturdays. Moments later, after the official opening, the pitch was invaded by the wives and families of the players and officials of the club and by the many helpers who had assisted in the backbreaking work involved.

Children's choir, 1912, with conductor John Thomas. On the right is Charles Graham Hughes the village schoolmaster.

Musical concert, Creigiau Church Hall, 1922. A combination of local and visiting talents gave high quality performances throughout the 1920s. The vicar, Revd Thomas Williams is seen standing at the far left and his wife, who was the producer, is on far right. Next but one to Mrs Williams is Peggy Llewellyn of Llwyndaddu, whose sister Kitty is on the far left of the second row from the back. The lady seated in the middle of the front row is Annie Jones, a star performer in all concerts.

Amongst the cultural 'activists' of the village, the Garth Gleemen, pictured here in 1932, occupied a prominent position. The party included men from all walks of life, mostly from Gwaelod y Garth, and under the leadership of W.J. George, won many trophies and took a special prize at the National Eisteddfod. The party rehearsed at Salem chapel and performed many concerts locally; they were a particular favourite of the US servicemen at Rhydlafar hospital.

The 'Sunbeams' of Salem chapel about 1920. This photograph is thought to be the only one taken of this children's drama group who performed in the vestry of Salem chapel, in both English and Welsh, and held their annual concert for the village in November.

Amateur dramatics played an important part in the life of Gwaelod y Garth village in the early twentieth century. The Garth Dramatic Society became well known in South Wales circles, winning several highly prestigious competitions, including those at Aberdare in 1915 and Treorchy in 1920. The two groups shown, although separated by over twenty-five years, illustrate the continuity of this aspect of village life, most of the participants being village residents.

'The Pentyrch Players', 1949. Amateur dramatics became very popular immediately after the war. The group put on regular productions in Pentyrch but were often invited to stage them in the surrounding villages as well. In this scene from one of Eynon Evans's comedies which played to a 'packed house' at St Catwg's Hall, we see, from left to right: Trefor Llewellyn, Caradog Evans, and Thomas Miles.

The cast of *Fresh Fields*, Pentyrch 1953. Standing: Don Llewellyn, Gwilym French, Ronnie Lawson, Edwina Jefferies, Philip Price, Dewi Thomas, Jim Rogers (producer), Lawrence Jefferies (actor and scenery builder). Seated: Joan Davies, Emmy Jenkins, Mary Bailey, Barbara Llewellyn, Rosie Zamastil, Jean Elliot, Florence Thomas. In front: Muriel Thomas, Beth Jenkins.

With very few people owning a vehicle in Gwaelod y Garth, and no public transport in the village until the late 1940s, an outing of any sort was a big occasion. The earlier photograph (about 1925) shows a charabanc about to leave for an unknown destination, while the later (about 1932) shows a mothers' trip to the seaside. Many of these outings were 'donated' by Mr Frazer of Creigiau.

Pentyrch point-to-point races, 1960. For many years, thousands of people came to this the biggest annual event in Pentyrch, where the soaring voices of over two dozen bookmakers competed with the sound of money changing hands. Running over Penllwyn and Pantygored land, the horses went briefly out of sight at the rise beyond Brista Fach; this gave an element of surprise when they returned to the view of the waiting punters. In the 1960s, however, the event moved to the Vale of Glamorgan.

Point-to-point, 1958. James Isaac (capless) on No Thoroughfare winning the Pentyrch Members' Race from Colin Davies on Master Copper.

Carnival day, Pentyrch, 1960. From left to right: Bill Perrett, Blodwen Jones, Nancy Howells, M. Davies, Hannah Jones, Horatio Thomas, 'Ma' Chamberlain.

Pentyrch cricket team, 1932. Back row: V. Pearce (umpire), T. Smith, T. Llewellyn, W. Lewis, D. Lewis, J. Thomas, A. Mathews, F. Davies, I. Stevens (umpire). Seated: E.T. Lewis (president), E.P. Evans, W. Stephens, S. Evans, W.J. Gibbs, A. Chamberlain (scorer). In front: R. Lawson, C. Lewis.

Gwaelod y Garth, 1945. Victory celebrations in the form of a street party and carnival were held to welcome the end of the Second World War. Both young and not so young turned out to provide a pageant of colour and ingenuity, particularly as at that time clothing was available only on production of the appropriate coupons. The young man with bare legs, left of centre, went appropriately as 'No coupons, no pants'.

High jinks on Bronllwyn Road, Pentyrch, 1932. On the stilts is Haydn Pulfrey with from left to right: A. David, Les Powles, Malgwyn Llewellyn, Sid Llewellyn, Idwal Stevens, Don Lindsay, Roy Wood.

Horeb Sunday school outing to Barry, 1935. At the back: Megan Griffiths, Mrs D. Griffiths, Doreen Treby, Marjorie Evans, Basil Evans, Hetty Phillips, Malgwyn Phillips, Mervyn Phillips, Mrs H. Treby, Lilian Treby, Dick Phillips, Ivor Phillips. In front: Mrs R. Williams with her arm around son Walter's shoulder, Joan Treby protected by Eddie Phillips, Ken Williams holding on to Ellis Davies, Betty Edwards with a case full of sandwiches, Edith Edwards, Doris Willicombe with Betty Phillips on her lap, Margaret Willicombe, Betty Willicombe, Megan Williams and Joan Williams.

Children playing on the 'Green', an area behind Glanyrafon, Gwaelod y Garth, which was well occupied on most summer evenings and at weekends. A big attraction was the 'Garth Rhondda' pond (named after the coal level), which became a swimming pool during the summer holidays and was often used by youngsters who 'could not afford swimming costumes'.

A Gwaelod y Garth gang, c. 1926. Children take time off from their activities to pose for a photograph, at the bottom of Salem Terrace. Salem field was well used as a playing field by children of all ages in the past, despite the occasional appearance of mysterious holes caused by the collapse of the underlying coal workings.

Celebrating a new king, Garth Mountain, 1911. The biggest bonfire ever seen on 'The Pimple' marked the coronation of George V and blazed for over two days. The pile was made from brushwood and bracken, an assortment of timbers including railway sleepers and unwanted household waste, all held in place by several obsolete rails brought from the old Pentyrch Ironworks yard. The inferno, assisted by barrels of pitch and oil-soaked rags, burned well into the first night lighting up the sky with a warm red glow. Forty-eight hours later, the embers still smouldered hotly. The many well-wishers reported that they could see similar celebratory fires on distant hills.

A gathering of the people on the Garth, 1927. On a cool morning, over two hundred residents of Pentyrch walked to 'The Pimple' on the Garth mountain to witness the eclipse of the sun. Many took the advice given in the *Western Mail* that in order to avoid damage to the eyes, the eclipse should be viewed only through a piece of smoked glass.

52

The King's Arms, Pentyrch – 'The Old
Pub'. In the seventeenth century it was a
copyhold farm called Cae Golman. For
two hundred years it was the main
gathering place for local singers and
poets. A long upstairs room was the
venue for concerts until it was changed
into living quarters in the 1950s. The
Oddfellows Society met there from the
1830s. The society's symbol showing a
large eye, a hand and a heart was
embedded in the ceiling. It carried the
legend: *Llygad i weled, llaw i gyfrannu a
chalon i deimlo* (an eye to behold, a hand
to contribute and a heart to sympathise).

Mrs Thomas with her daughter
Susannah at their home the Rock and
Castle public house, Pentyrch, 1900.

Creigiau Hotel, 1908. A thriving Temperance Hotel during Creigiau's early years when cycling was fashionable and the railway brought hordes of walkers and picnickers to the area. In the middle years of the century, Captain Dark ran a popular club on the premises.

On a sunny summer's day such as this Edwardian ladies could take refreshments in the tea garden at the hotel. They had probably parked their bikes out of sight.

James Williams, Thomas Jones and Thomas Hearn pose outside the Gwaelod y Garth inn c. 1900. The landlord at that time was Manoah Morgan, an ex-collier, who kept the inn from 1895 to about 1916. The earliest census reference to the inn is 1851 when the landlord was John Lewis.

Manoah Morgan with one of his staff, or possibly his wife.

The Lewis Arms, 1902. It would be logical to assume that the authoritative-looking gentleman in the centre is the landlord of the public house. However, he bears no resemblance to Evan Evans who kept the Lewis Arms at the time. It is thought by some to be William Evans of the village store (out of picture to the left). Certainly the haltered horse is someone's prize possession and the photographer, on his way through the village building up his 'picture postcard' collection, arrived at a good moment. The Lewis Arms was built in the early 1850s by Job Williams of Y Gocyd.

Y Twyn, 1905. This natural mound was a favourite gathering place and playground for locals and picnickers from afar. The site of the old lime kiln used by Penygarn farm was levelled in the 1940s to make a car park for the Lewis Arms public house.

The Colliers' Arms, 1930. A three-storey house was built adjoining the public house which was not as isolated as it looks, for nearby on the breast of the mountain was a small community. However, no longer having the trade it used to enjoy when the nearby drift mines were active, the pub survived for only a few more years. In its heyday in the last century, it was a favourite venue for concerts and eisteddfodau.

Carnival Day in Pentyrch, 1963. The Women's Institute and the Women's Whist Guild could always be relied upon to enter into the spirit of the local carnival.

Bagpipe and organ player, 1900. Strolling musicians, including harpists, tin whistle and banjo players, were still a common sight in Pentyrch at the turn of the century continuing their visits up to the First World War. The piper plays before the barn at Penygarn farm in Heol Goch, the organ grinder outside the Villa in Temperance Road.

Teetotallers' outing, 1904. Nine of the group are Pentyrch rugby players. Several who had been affected by the recent religious revival remained abstinent throughout their lives, a few did not! It was a proud boast of the rugby club that most of their members were staunch teetotallers.

Four

Learning

Few aspects of past times in Pentyrch could be considered without reference to the pioneering monk who founded the place. Catwg, who was himself a teacher, illuminated his time with many sayings, several of which touch upon the need for learning. Whilst he regarded the pursuit of knowledge as a virtuous act, he taught that the acquisition of wisdom was an even more blessed function in life. His own sagacity was much celebrated, as indeed were his chastity, his humanity, his sense of justice and his independent spirit. The centuries have resounded with the endeavours of the local populace trying to emulate the virtuous Catwg, some persons running him close, others, it must be said, failing hopelessly!

In the oral tradition each century had its roll-call of 'wise' persons and educational leaders; there are also impressive examples of academic success achieved by those who began their learning in the parish. Among the most notable of the latter was one John Jones, the son of Mathew Jones of Pentyrch. He was entered at Jesus College Oxford in 1672, being then seventeen years of age and later became a fellow. Having taken his degree in arts, he studied law and was admitted doctor of that faculty in 1677. He practised physic at Windsor and in 1691 he was made chancellor of Llandaff. He was a man of ingenuity as well as learning: in 1683, he published a Latin treatise on intermittent fevers. According to Plot's Natural History of Oxfordshire, he invented a clock which moved by the air, equally expressed out of bellows of a cylindrical form, which fell into folds in its descent. He died in 1709.

In 1740 Pentyrch had one of the Griffith Jones circulating schools teaching men and women to 'read God's holy word in their native British tongue'. Forty years later local industrialists, in particular the Quaker ironmasters, were providing some daily education for their employees' children. Starting with Horeb in 1804, Sunday schools established by the chapels flourished and in 1834 the Church established a National school. Pentyrch did not escape Brâd y Llyfrau Gleision (The Treachery of the Blue Books). The 1847 Report of the Commissioners of Enquiry into the state of Education in Wales cruelly misinterpreted the monoglot Welsh fluency of pupils, mistaking it for illiteracy.

It took ten years for a School Board to be formed in Pentyrch after the Education Act of 1870 but the new system eventually settled well into the existing church school. This and the other seat of learning at Bethlehem, Gwaelod y Garth produced a stream of successful pupils who went on to make their mark in the wider world. The present school building at Gwaelod y Garth was built in the 1880s whereas the Pentyrch Council School was not opened until 1907. The 1950s saw the closing of an era when 'John Willie Evans' of Creigiau passed away bringing his small but extraordinarily successful private school to an end.

The site of the original chapel and school at Gwaelod y Garth. It was originally set up as a circulating school in about 1829 on weekdays and as a chapel on Sundays. Largely funded by the Melingriffith Company, it was still in use as a school in the 1890s, the existing Gwaelod y Garth school having commenced in 1881, the larger building being added in 1898. Its use as a chapel ceased with the opening of Capel Bethlehem in 1872, and it is now a private residence.

The staff of the Gwaelod y Garth school in 1893. The headmaster, Mr Alfred Roberts, is seated in the centre. Second from the right in the back row is Lizzie Roblin, a pupil teacher, who later became Mrs Christopher and whose great-grandchildren still live in the village. Also in the picture is Mary Persis Thomas, latterly known as 'Mrs Thomas the Shop'. It is recorded in the school log at the time that 'the attendance [in September] was dreadful as many children took time off to pick blackberries and nuts, and sold them for money'.

A class of the Bethlehem school in 1875. This group is outside the original school, before the opening of the Board school in Gwaelod y Garth in 1881. The school was partly funded by the owners of the ironworks and was attended by children from outside the village on payment of a weekly fee of two pence. The headmaster shown is Mr Thomas Madge.

Gwaelod y Garth Standard IV, 1912.

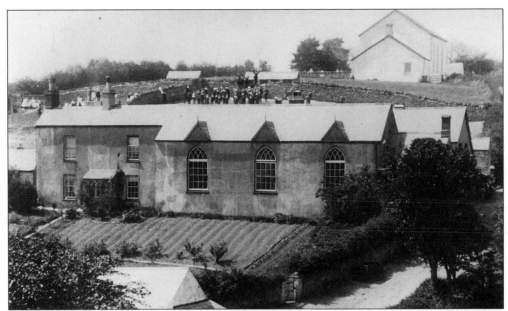

Pentyrch Board School, 1896. The building had for several decades housed the local National school under the auspices of the parish church. It took some time for the Education Act of 1870 to take effect since it was 1880 before the Pentyrch School Board was established. Eventually, the demands of compulsory education caused overcrowding and led to temporary accommodation being arranged at Penuel Baptist chapel on the hill above. After the new council school was opened in the village in 1907 the building, then called St Catwg's Hall served as a venue for concerts, drama productions and dances until it was demolished in the early 1970s to make way for the houses known as Cefn Llan.

The crossroads at Penybyrdir, 1907. The newly opened council school (left) catered for children who lived within a radius of three miles. With no motor vehicles to trouble them, these young people could wander down Bronllwyn Road at will.

School group, 1893 – a picture of the older children dressed up for a play, concert, or some celebratory event. Suggestive of Gilbert and Sullivan; was it for a *Mikado* performance? Taken in the field next to Tŷ Gwellt across the road from the Board school, the outline of Caerwal farmhouse can be seen on the skyline. Each boy holds a fan; the girls, in laced up shoes and sporting the odd cameo brooch, are all in identical white dresses. Each girl carries a doll, has a bunch of daisies in her hand, with the dolls similarly bedecked. Mr Charles Graham Hughes the schoolmaster and the lady teacher at the other end of the group carry fans. Mr Jones ('Jones bach') the headmaster, holds a baton, or is it a cane? Note the younger boy, not part of the group, peering through the hedge!

Details from the school group. Above: Theresa and Idwal John. Below: Susannah Thomas of the Rock and Castle with Gwilym David. Right: a typical girl and boy from the group.

Pentyrch school hockey players, 1909. The new school had been opened just two years and there was a growing emphasis on sporting pursuits for both girls and boys. The girls played hockey on the Dwrlyn fields. A decade later, boys of the school, much to their regret, were forced to play association football instead of rugby which had the stronger tradition in the village.

Cookery class, Pentyrch school, 1912. From left to right: Gwladys Wheeler, Evelyn Ingles, Mrs Edwards (teacher), Winnie Jones, Martha Rees, behind her (head only showing) Hattie Basham, Margaret Evans, H. Adams (in the background is Latia Thomas), Margery Sparks, Kitty Lewis, (head showing behind unknown), -?-, Kitty Llewellyn (still living in Creigiau), Maud Sparks, May Evans, Maggie Llewellyn.

Infants at Pentyrch school, 1909. On the right is pupil teacher Miss Bessie Watkins of The Warren.

Pentyrch school, standards III and IV, 1914. The schoolmaster is Mr Charles Graham Hughes ('Bottlebelly Punch').

Pentyrch school infants class, 1933. Top row: David Evans, Glyn Rogers, Norman Follis, Vivian Noakes, Arthur Llewellyn, Ronald Boots, John Diment. Middle row: Dora Howe, Beryl Gibbs, Megan Thomas, Lilian Organ, Lilian Hunter, Phyllis Hawkins, Donald Ham. Bottom row: Nesta Llewellyn, Derek Murphy, Mervyn Thomas, Mair Phillips, Vera French, Eric Wheeler.

Pentyrch school headmaster David Williams ('Dai Bill') and teacher Stanley ('Dickie') Moore with successful scholarship pupils in 1937. Back row: Dilwyn Pritchard and Roy Davies (Caerphilly Tech.), Roy Lewis and Basil Evans (Whitchurch High). Front row: Jenny Williams, Louie Thomas and Doris Willicombe (Whitchurch High).

Nine sturdy boys with a day off from school possibly to go beating at a local pheasant shoot. Top left, back row Evan Jenkins ('Ianto Crydd'), third left Idris Llewellyn ('Cock Robin') and far right Evan Christopher. Front row: B. Beer, Henry Llewellyn, Francis Llewellyn and Wil Hodges.

Many schoolchildren and their teachers were evacuated to the parish during the early part of the Second World War. Here, Gwaelod y Garth boys pose with a Miss Pat Grimley after a swimming lesson at Taff's Well baths in 1941. From left to right (on wall): Arthur Boobier, Emlyn Davies, John Tyler, Johnny Thomas. In front: Dennis Luxton, Les George.

The private school of John 'Willie' Evans, Creigiau, 1930. At back: Edward Llewellyn, Lewis Bassett. Middle row: Deborah Jones, Francis Brown, Stephanie Phillips, Mr Evans, Eluned Thomas, Owen Davies, Olive Bassett. In front: Lettie Davies. The schoolmaster was the oldest son of William and Jennet Evans of Penygarn Stores, Pentyrch. Educated at Colston's School in Bristol and then Oxford, he returned to teach local children at his small day school in Creigiau. A learned man with a knowledge of the classics, he could speak several languages fluently, in addition to Welsh, his mother tongue. John Willie died in 1951, aged eighty-two, and there are still many who treasure memories of the kindness that underlay his stern discipline.

Gwaelod y Garth infants class, 1947. The senior lady is Miss Gwladys Foxall who taught in the school for many years and was known as 'Governess'.

Five

Rural Life

Within the boundaries of the old parish of Pentyrch there is a remarkably wide range of terrain. As the land climbs to the north, it leaves behind the pastures which belong in character to the Vale of Glamorgan. By the time it reaches the windswept Garth ridge, meadow gives way to moorland. Woods comprising predominantly oak, ash, beech and birch stand neatly on many slopes throughout the parish and streamlets trickle down eastwards to the River Taff and to the Ely valley in the west. The agricultural tradition was strong through the centuries and the Trethiant Plwyf Pentyrch valuation of 1825 reveals that there were nearly four score farmsteads and smallholdings active at that time. For a period, the rich resources of iron and coal in the locality posed a threat to the countryside but this was comparatively short-lived. Traces of the industrial enterprises which were a feature of the eastern side of the parish in the eighteenth and nineteenth centuries have all but gone and even substantial new residential developments have failed to destroy the parish's essentially rural identity. Today, modern farming methods enable a few to carry on the tradition of high quality land husbandry and stock raising, even on what used to be considered poor ground. Whilst only echoes of some of the more ancient aspects of rural life remain, there is an awareness among the present inhabitants that what is left should be preserved and that our precious open spaces should be defended.

The village store of Mr Charles Seale, 1934. In addition to serving the small community of Creigiau with groceries, it sold ironmongery including household utensils and gardening tools. Bread and cakes baked on the premises were delivered by his son Mr Percy Seale to outlying farms and parts of Pentyrch as well as Creigiau itself. The shop was situated where the Creigiau Stores and Post Office now stand. The Seales ran the shop from 1925 until 1946.

Temperance Road, 1903. A pony and trap awaits the ladies of Bronllwyn Villa, possibly to take them to Cardiff.

'Dafydd y töwr gwellt' (the thatcher) on his rounds, 1899. There was still plenty of work for Dafydd at the turn of the century: in Pentyrch parish there were more than sixty dwellings with thatched roofs. The slate-roofed building here is Maesteg barn on Tyncoed Road, the present home of Pentyrch foxhounds.

Cwm Llwydrew, 1958. The valley had regained its rural beauty; no trace could be seen of either the old drift down at Coed y Bedw or the spots where coal had been picked out of the Garth half a century earlier. The Colliers' Arms had gone and so had the cottages which stood on the eastern slopes of the mountain. Caerwen farm (top left) was still active but the perpetually burning field to which Malkin refers in his tour account of 1803 had long since cooled.

This stone at a lonely spot on the windswept Garth mountain is one of the great local mysteries. In the oral tradition it is said to mark the unconsecrated burial place of a sixteenth-century witch called Mari Cabbitsan. In one account, for stealing a sheep, she was said to have been executed by hanging in the barn of Ffrwd Meurig farm near the Colliers' Arms. The story of 'Mary Ann Cabbage' has been fancifully embellished over the years.

This magnificent view from a postcard produced about 1900, includes the principal buildings in the 'Old Village'. On higher ground much of the Penygarn area, the highest house in the parish, Ty'n y Ffald, and the 'Pimple' are prominent.

Penygarn farm, 1962, just before renovation. William Llewellyn who farmed here in the nineteenth century was also a builder and a noted butcher. Some of his several sons kept up the family tradition in the meat trade and farming in Pentyrch.

72

Castell y Mynach was neither a castle nor a monastery. The earliest known form of the name – 'Menach' – shows that it was current before Welsh evolved from the British Celtic language. Any monkish association with the site therefore dates from early post-Roman times. Built by Robert ap Mathew in the early fifteenth century, the oldest part of the present house is the east wing, originally a ground floor hall, open to the surviving wind-braced roof. The Mathew family lived here for eleven generations until the end of the seventeenth century. The Royal Stuart coat of arms in the hall supports the local legend that King Charles visited here.

Pantygored, 1910, was built in the late fifteenth century by John ap Thomas, a descendent of Llywelyn ap Cynwrig whose family held a lease of Pentyrch Manor. His daughter and heiress married Robert Mathew of Castell y Mynach, combining the two estates after which Pantygored was a tenanted farmhouse. The thatched roof survived until the late 1940s. One of the most historically important houses in the area, it has now been well restored, with many old features revealed. The 'cored' or weir from which the house takes its name would have been on nearby Nant Gilaswg, creating a fishpond.

Tŷ Gwellt, Pentyrch, 1894. Perhaps the lady is waiting for callers who might require the soft drinks which were sold at the house on hot summer days to visitors to the churchyard opposite. The cottages at the top right are vacant and awaiting conversion work which would produce the new English Mission Hall the following year.

Gilaswg, Pentyrch, 1899. This picturesque cottage stood alongside the road to Creigiau near the 'waterworks' and was occupied until the 1930s. The road passed the other side of the house until it was diverted during the last quarter of the nineteenth century. Typical of the seventeenth-century dwellings, it was one-roomed and storeyed. Until relatively recently thatch was the universal roofing material in Pentyrch.

Brista Fach, 1899. One of two adjacent eighteenth-century farmhouses. Founded in 1740, the Pentyrch Methodist Society was based here, before moving to Horeb in 1838. Earlier the building was part of a commercially important hamlet and its name arose from the stocking of leather, supplied from Bristol, for the use of local shoemakers. It had also been an alehouse. In a 1637/8 Manor Court Roll, Thomas ap John of Brista Fach was fined 2/6d for selling less than the lawful measure. In the 1930s half the property was destroyed by fire.

Ffynnon Dwym, Creigiau 1905. Taking its name from a nearby 'warm' well which is said to have curative properties, it is another of the several one-roomed, storeyed farmhouses built in Pentyrch during the seventeenth century but later reduced to cottager status. This house was finally abandoned in the 1930s after which it burned down. Morgan Watcyn, the legendary mole-catcher, lived here in 1841.

High Corner, Pentyrch, 1898. These delightful single-storey cottages stood where the road turns towards the mountain near the present village centre. The tips of Post Office Terrace and Cambria Terrace can just be seen. The waste ground was called 'the old buildings' long after the cottages were knocked down and removed.

Blaenbielli, 1900 – an early Pentyrch farm on the approaches to the Garth. Notable occupants include Evan John senior (Ifan Siôn), agent for the estate during the last century. Later, David Richards, a 'giant' of the Bronllwyn congregation resided there. It is said that he could not be disturbed while he sat for three hours every night at the kitchen table reading the Holy Book by candlelight. For most of the first half of the present century it was farmed by George Llewellyn, of Penygarn stock. People believed that rain would inevitably follow his mowing of the main field in front of Blaenbielli and if locals saw him harnessing up the mare to the reaper, they planned their day accordingly.

Ploughing at Penllwyn, 1940. During the Second World War more land than ever fell to the plough. George Jones was a skilful ploughman and like many local farmers of the time, was adept at using a harnessed pair. Soon though, the rumble of tractors would become a common sound in the village.

Penllwyn rickyard, 1938. The method of harvesting and storing hay had changed little over many centuries. The guarantee of mutual help was still a bond which held the farming community together.

Cefn Colstyn, Pentyrch, 1899. First recorded as a copyhold farm in 1570 belonging to one Griffith Jevan Morgan, it then probably comprised little more than fifteen or twenty acres. By 1839 it had absorbed numerous neighbouring copyholds and much manorial demesne land to become one of the largest farms in the parish and part of the Castell y Mynach estate.

Family group of John Williams who farmed Cefn Colstyn from the turn of the century. Sadly, Mrs Williams (née Joan Roberts of Garth farm) passed away at the age of thirty-nine after having borne ten children. Some of the offspring stayed with farming, others did not. Standing in the centre is Tom Williams who became an actor. On the right is his younger brother Robert who went on to farm at Caerphilly. John the younger, centre front, succeeded his father at Cefn Colstyn. Elizabeth on the right wed Davy Evans of Penllwyn. On the left is Catherine who married Tom Llewellyn of Rhydlafar and was the mother of the present owner of Cefn Colstyn.

Caerarfau, a farmhouse built or, more likely, rebuilt in 1672. After being combined with neighbouring Cefn Gwarwig to form a farm of about 90 acres, the homestead was enlarged. The roof was raised in the nineteenth century to give full headroom in the bedrooms which would originally have been partly in the roof. Although the date-plate above the door says 1672, the local oral tradition links Caerarfau with the Civil War three decades earlier. Pentyrch's oldest man-made structure, a cromlech, stands within its grounds.

Llwynybrain Mawr (Grove of the Crows), a seventeenth-century farmhouse. A local legend claims that a boy, guarding the corn, shot at crows using nails and tacks which pinned the birds to the branches of a tree. The crows uprooted the tree and flew away with it to Hereford. There some brown cattle were so shocked by the arrival of the tree that their faces turned white. Thus the breed of 'White-faced Herefords' began!

'Jones the butcher', 1938 – Cadwgan Jones at his shop which stood in Temperance Road until the 1960s. Born at Penllwyn, which has historical associations with the thirteenth-century warrior Cadwgan Fawr, the butcher was appropriately named.

Cefn Bychan, Pentyrch, 1920. From left to right: Harry Llewellyn (Penygarn), Wyndham and Ned Davies (Caerwal). Pork and bacon were very popular but the animals themselves were often revered personalities in their own right. Verses written by Oliver Prichard describing the 'funeral' of a much admired pig in 1898 confirm the status enjoyed by these prized possessions:

Mae holl trigolion Cefn Bychan wedi cael eu taro'n syn
Trwy i angeu ddod mor sydyn a thori lawr y mochyn gwyn
Gweithiwr tlawd yr oedd ei berchen, Ben Drescythan ydoedd e
Gwnewch gydymddwyn trwy rhoddi arian i gael mochyn yn ei le.
Yn ei angladd 'roedd personau, boneddigion pena'r wlad:
William Prichard, Betasea a William Gruffydd yr hen dad
Jim gwr Rhoda, Ben Drescythan, Wil ei frawd a Twm Ton Mawr
Oli Lisa, Dai mab Letis, dyna eu henwau'n drefnus 'nawr.

Hay making at Penygarn farm, 1935. Cymro the cob is in the shafts of a 'gambo', a two-wheeled Welsh cart used in Pentyrch. From the left: farmer Lewis Llewellyn, son of William the Victorian butcher, Stan Richards, Gwilym Edmunds, a knowledgeable countryman who kept ferrets, bred terriers, budgerigars and racing pigeons. Two-year-old Raymond Llewellyn is with his father Evan next to Sid ('Bonzo') Evans.

John Foster Lloyd, who kept the post office and general store in Gwaelod y Garth from about 1909 until after the Second World War, poses proudly with his new delivery vehicle. The building in the background, now the site of a modern bungalow, was formerly a bakehouse, providing most of the village with its bread.

Creigiau farm, 1905. The farmhouse to which the new village of Creigiau owed its name had been rebuilt by the estate in 1820. Before the railway station was erected on its land, the farm was known simply as Criga, Pentyrch. Mr Trevor Davies who worked the farm until the 1950s was one of the last in the area to use a horse-drawn milk float for delivery.

Cefn Gwarwig, 1900. A cottage alongside the railway on what was then Caerarfau farm. Still occupied in the present century, it was typical of local storeyed stone farmhouses built in the seventeenth century. When its thirty or so acres were combined with Caerarfau, this house remained unaltered, a labourer's cottage for another two hundred years.

Cefn Bychan farm and Brynhyfryd, 1904. This was a route out of Pentyrch to Radyr for centuries and was the original Heol Goch. The road was diverted lower down at Cwmllwydrew to become 'Pentyrch Hill' in 1885. The area beyond the farm, before the old lane dips towards the valley, is still known as Graig Goch. The farmhouse, part of which dates from the middle 1500s, is one of the oldest inhabited houses in the area.

Llwynyreos, Pentyrch, 1950. David Williams alias David Edmund died here in 1833. His father's name was Edmund [ap] Richard and his son William adopted the name David/Davies. It took another generation to establish itself and is the latest known example of surname formation in the parish. He left the lease of Llwynyreos to his daughter Ann, the wife of Edward Rees whose descendants lived here throughout the nineteenth century, claiming Pentyrch ancestry dating from a period earlier than that of Catwg himself!

Looking westwards from Mountain Road near Y Gwattan, 1900. Meadow Cottage (Tŷ Bili Shinco) also possibly the site of Ty Mary Evan and Graig y Moel farm mentioned in early leases, Tŷ Llwyd, Mountain Ash Cottage and Y Warren can be seen. On the horizon is Silver Brook (Nant yr Arian) where Mr J.L. Wheatley, Clerk to Cardiff Town Council, then resided. If the youngsters were gathering firewood for Siân Watcyn's oven they had better be ash sticks for the good lady would accept no other kind. This fact was said to be the reason for her legendary success in baking bread.

Caerwal Terrace, 1898. Also called Quarry Row and Field Terrace in the past, it has been known as Field Row for most of this century. In the middle of the terrace Dai Lee kept his greengrocer's shop. The first property on the right is where Edwin Gardner sold fish and chips in the 1930s; in more recent times it was the Elms family's butcher's shop.

A view of the top end of Gwaelod y Garth village about 1910. Of interest is the alignment of Ffigys House, believed to be the old Ffigys farmhouse seen on the far right that occupied this site from about 1820 to 1881. The houses shown were built about 1845 on land belonging to the farm then owned by the Melingriffith Company which, on its collapse in 1881, sold the freehold to Wingfield estates

A view of the road through Gwaelod y Garth. This photograph was taken from near the hotel, probably about the same time as that above.

Penllwyn, 1900. Now consumed by Creigiau quarry, this typical farmstead, largely a nineteenth-century rebuild, stood near the medieval seat of one Cynfyn Fychan ap Cynfyn ap Genillon ap Rhys Goch, Prince of Ystrad Yw, who 'with divers kinsmen having escaped from the strangers that then possessed Ystrad Yw ... were gratefully received in the Lordship of Meisgyn then also distressed by incursions of strangers then possessing the low country of Glamorgan. The said Cynfyn possessed the lands in Meisgyn after his name called Penllwyn Cynfyn'.

Maesteg farmhouse, 1900. When the northern perimeter of Creigiau quarry was extended in the 1950s, this farm was removed from the map; a hundred feet deep cliff face now exists where the farmhouse stood. A small parcel, the land was farmed in the first half of this century by Tom Morgan and his sister Hannah, raising cattle, sheep, ducks and geese.

Garth Cottages, 1905. Little Sue Evans with her mother Elizabeth and her aunty, Bopa Williams.

Garth Uchaf, Pentyrch, 1955. In the thirteenth century, under better climatic conditions, this was an open field on which grain was being grown by a bond community belonging to Hywel ap Meredudd, the last Welsh lord of Meisgyn. It was a freehold, stock-raising farm in the 1500s known as Tir Evan ap Jenkin. Two hundred years later Evan's descendant, William Nichol, a Dissenter, was fined for non-payment of tithes; perhaps it was he who built the chapel said to have been at nearby Soar. His son of the same name fled to Ireland after being accused of two murders. The latter's heiress married Mr Bassett of Bonvilston whose descendants still held Garth Uchaf in the nineteenth century. The Pentyrch hounds were kennelled here for many years in this century.

Llwyndaddu, 1955. On the southern ridgeway of Pentyrch overlooking the vale of Ely, it is a site of ancient occupation. There was a small Iron Age fort, or defended homestead close by the present house. Iolo Morganwg perpetuated an unlikely local claim that a medieval teacher from Flintshire, Dafydd Ddu, Athro o Hiraddug kept a school here and gave his name to the farm. Among the other traditions is one that links clock making with Llwyndaddu, hence the thought that the seventeenth-century scholar John Jones of Pentyrch had lived there, for besides his reputation in medicine, he is said to have invented a timepiece which worked by means of air passing through bellows.

Penllwyn, 1960. The eighteenth-century barn shows the past prosperity of this farm. The last tenant before the quarry took over the land was Mr George Jones who said that the date 1795 was burnt into one of the timbers. Mr Jones claimed descent from Cadwgan Fawr, a descendant of Cynfyn through a branch of that family that had settled in Ystradyfodwg. Cadwgan Fawr himself, though commonly associated with Ystradyfodwg, probably lived in Pentyrch where local tradition holds that he died. His cry *Hoga'r fwyall* (Sharpen the axe) inspired his warriors in the defence of his domain which explains why the name 'Cadwgan' remained a metaphor in Pentyrch for an axe until the last century. Bulls at Penllwyn often carried the name. George Jones, who had heard of the historical connection realised the significance of one of his brothers bearing the name Cadwgan.

A view of upper Gwaelod in the 1940s. The buildings on the left include a veal slaughterhouse – the cottage opposite being a butchers' shop. The figure in the mid-distance is possibly collecting water from the communal village pump, which was opposite the post office – one of four pumps which supplied all of the houses on the main road.

Yr Efail, Pentyrch, 1899. The smithy at Maes y Gof where, for forty years from 1855, William Mathews ('Wil y Gof') shod horses, mended carts, made gates and repaired countless iron and steel implements for the local farming community. He brought coal to Penygarn from Pantygored Sidings, twenty-five donkeys carrying it in panniers.

Shearing sheep at Pantygored, 1925. The tradition of mutual help among farmers had not died out and the first to arrive this shearing day were, far left, James Davies of Creigiau farm standing alongside Tom Jones of Llwynioli. Their sons Willie Jones and Trevor Davies are the white-shirted pair at the back, kneeling. Standing in the centre of the photograph is Ted Watts.

An early recruit to the Women's Land Army, Irene Marshall from Barry arrived at Creigiau farm at the end of 1939. Previously unaccustomed to farm work, she learned a variety of jobs quickly and ably. Mr and Mrs Trevor Davies rated her work highly and were sad when she had to leave after a year at their farm. It was government policy to move the girls around as much as possible. In Irene's case it was a posting to Worcester.

Tŷ Gwellt, at the top of Rock Hill and the foot of Penuel Hill, 1927. The dwelling was one of a cluster of thatched cottages in the vicinity of the church and the 'Old School'. The seventeenth-century structure was still sound when it was demolished in 1959 but the thatch was in need of renewal.

Upper Pentyrch (Penygarn), June 1954. Possibly the last photograph of this view to be taken before work on the council house development commenced at Berthlwyd, Danyrodyn and Heol y Pentre and before the private housing estates took over the area in the foreground. The scene is still essentially rustic as Austin Thomas the farmer of Ty'nycoed farm, adjacent to the church, brings in a good crop of hay. The rural setting was destined not to last, for in time 240 houses would be built on these fields.

Neighbours at Cambria Terrace, 1938. Standing, foreground: Mrs Esther Jones and Mrs Selina Davies. In front: Mrs S. Lewis. In background: Mrs Margaret Llewelyn and Herbert Jones.

Dr D. Thomas, otherwise known (affectionately) as 'Bread Poultice'. Based in Radyr and Morganstown, this West Walian doctor was pleased that his practice took him to Pentyrch, where the vast majority of his patients were Welsh speaking. He became a local legend due to his jolly manner and the regularity with which he recommended the consumption of milk puddings and the application of bread poultices to affected parts! It earned him the sobriquet of which, it is said, he was very proud and would laugh loudly when it was mentioned in his presence. On one occasion, he was carrying his bicycle across the footbridge from Taff's Well after one of his tyre inner tubes had suffered a blow-out. Referring to the rubber bubble growing by the minute from the tyre, a group of local lads shouted some inevitable advice to the physician: 'Put a poultice on it doctor! Put a poultice on it!'.

Six
Village People

It has been said that the feeling of belonging to a particular place is a recognised characteristic of the Welsh. One's 'own patch' (y milltir scwar – the square mile) around the place of birth and in some cases even an adoptive home has a magnetic effect that seems less potent among other peoples. While we travel the world as much as others, it is we who are pulled homeward by that unbearable hiraeth which loses something in the translation when described simply as 'longing'. It has certainly been a trait in the personality of those Pentyrch people who have deep roots in the parish. More interestingly, it has been seen to have affected newcomers as well, and these days it is the newly arrived residents who are often the most vociferous and ardent defenders of their 'place'. It would take many volumes to mention even a fraction of the number of people who have shown conspicuous pride in 'belonging' to the ancient parish. The following is a minute and purely random collection of those who have graced our villages in the past.

Golden wedding, 1900. Some of the family of Enoc Dafydd and his wife Mariah. Welsh was the first language of all of the figures in this photograph whilst this great village patriarch, like several others of his family, had no English. The local *dyn dŵr* (waterman) was a familiar figure striding through Pentyrch ensuring that the supply flowed freely from the new Garth reservoir. A devout Calvinistic Methodist worshipping at Horeb, he carried his faith into all aspects of his life, no doubt bolstered by the fact that he emerged victorious from a number of verbal confrontations with the Devil whom he claimed to have met on the mountain road!

Unveiling of the War Memorial, 17 July 1921. The monument raised by public subscription to the memory of the fifteen from the parish who fell in the First World War was unveiled by Thomas Evans JP, CBE of Craig y Parc. Erected on a site presented by Colonel Henry Lewis JP of Greenmeadow, the memorial was dedicated by Revd Thomas Williams vicar of the parish. Eloquent addresses were given in Welsh by Revd R G Berry and Councillor John Phillips JP and followed in English by Lieutenant-Colonel M.E.G.R. Wingfield. The Garth Male Voice Choir gave a moving rendering of *Peace to the Souls of the Heroes* and the service was brought to a close with a prayer by Revd J.E. Davies and the sounding of *The Last Post*. The memorial, of Cornish grey granite, was designed by Mr James Grey West of Pentyrch and executed by Mr Morgan Williams, sculptor of Taff's Well.

Following the Second World War the names of the fourteen who perished in that conflict were added to the memorial at another dignified bilingual ceremony. John Phillips JP was present again, this time accompanied by the vicar of Pentyrch, Revd Wilfred Lewis and other ministers. Once again as heads were bowed, it was the haunting tones of a bugler sounding a lament for the fallen, which brought the solemn proceedings to an end.

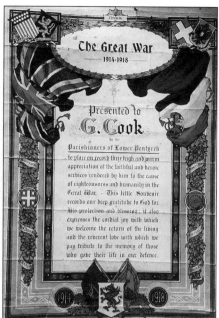

Mr George Cook, formerly of the Welch regiment whose grandchildren and great-grandchildren still live in Gwaelod y Garth, together with the certificate presented to him by the 'Parishioners of Lower Pentyrch' on his safe return from the battlefields of the First World War.

Two sailors in the Second World War. Kenneth Sparkes, a Creigiau boy was rescued after the destroyer *Ghurka* was sunk by a German aircraft. Edgar Davies of Pentyrch (pictured here wearing cap of Plymouth training establishment HMS *Drake*) lost his life when the anti-aircraft cruiser *Bonaventure* was torpedoed on 31 March 1941 off Crete in the eastern Mediterranean.

Mounted Home Guard, 1942. Farmers from Pentyrch and district were keen members of the Radyr and Morganstown Platoon which had its HQ at Radyr Golf Club. From left to right: George Loveluck (Rhydlafar), George Jones (Penllwyn), Jack Watkins (Cwm), Trevor Davies (Creigiau), John Evans (Tŷ Du), Aubrey Rees (Forty), Bill Richards (Radyr), Thurston Wride (Waterhall), George Bale (Gelynis), Alban Francis (Stockland) and Doc Steele.

FIRED BY NAZI RAIDER

Woodlands, Pantygored Road, Creigiau, July 1942. 'That night there were 13 blazing incendiaries in our garden. My mother was racing in and out with the stirrup pump and buckets of water. Confined beneath the stairs with Mrs Morris our lodger, I was praying. Then the cry went up that Woodlands was ablaze. Next morning it was a smouldering shell. Neighbours (from where did so many spring?) were salvaging furniture and Mrs Davies, surrounded by local matrons was sitting in Mrs Morgan's kitchen drinking tea and sympathy. They say several cattle were killed St Fagans way. Having an air-raid was not believed as an excuse for missing school that day for there had been no raid on Cardiff. During my enforced day off I found in our garden a further seven bombs which had not detonated.'

Thomas Williams, 1875. One of sixteen children of Evan Williams of Gocyd Uchaf, Tom lived his whole life (1810 to 1897) in Pentyrch. His mother's father was Evan Morgan of Craig Gwilym, renter of Tyncoed's coal measures. As a contractor, Tom built thirteen chapels and with his brother John, constructed lengths of the Taff Vale Railway and Aberdare branch line. He lived at Cwmfuwch and with his wife and thirteen children, worshipped at Taihirion. His wife Sarah had been a member there since maidenhood. With tears running down his cheeks he would often describe his own conversion which had taken place during the revival of 1859. When he erected Bronllwyn chapel, he also built Bronllwyn Villa where he lived out his last days.

Charles Prichard (1824-1912). Born in Merthyr Tydfil, Charles Prichard came to Pentyrch as a young man and quickly fell in love with the place and its traditions. He was a local schoolmaster for thirty-six years and for over half a century controlled and distributed assistance to the poor in his position as assistant overseer for the parish. His influence on the local community in the Victorian period was immense. For over sixty years he was secretary of the local lodge of the Independent Order of Oddfellows and was an ardent campaigner for all social, cultural and educational causes which affected the lives of working people. He also ran a small private academy at Brynteg House where a few villagers learned some English under his guidance.

Job Williams, 1878. Carpenter, builder, farmer, undertaker and deacon at Horeb, he died at Gocyd Uchaf where he was born. Briefly, when first married he kept the Bute Arms public house in the Old Village (at Bro Nant). He also built the Lewis Arms, later modernised by his son-in-law. He built Horeb chapel as it now stands; the original structure was built by his eldest brother Evan of Baily Coch in 1838. He was persuaded to cease being the landlord of the Lewis Arms by his fellow deacons at Horeb.

Eleanor Williams, 1878. Wife of Job Williams of Gocyd Uchaf and daughter of William Evans, blacksmith and innkeeper of the Walnut Tree near what is now Taff's Well. As a girl she attended a school in Whitchurch and Mr Charles Prichard, the Pentyrch schoolmaster is reported to have said that she was the only woman in Pentyrch who could speak English.

The young Thomas Henry Sparks with his grandmother in 1874. She was Ann the daughter of Edward Rees of Llwynyreos in Pentyrch and it was her claim that her family was the oldest in the parish. They descended, so she insisted, from Ceinwen who was a contemporary of St Gwladus, the mother of St Catwg.

Sparks 'Y Gocyd', 1938. Thomas Henry Sparks JP lived all his 87 years in Pentyrch and was many years a churchwarden. His grandfather had been coachman to Horatio Thomas the illustrious vicar. Thomas Henry's deep attachment to St Catwg's led to his donation in 1944 of the lych-gate which he had himself designed. A carpenter by trade, he married his boss's daughter, inherited the family building business, articled himself and qualified as an architect and surveyor. Working for the Ely Brewery, he converted their houses to mock Tudor, a style he also imposed upon much of the 'Old Village'. His many contributions to life in the community included the chairmanship of Cardiff Rural District Council.

Joshua Jenkins of Efail y Castell was the Creigiau postman. He was a popular local character who cheerfully put up with the constraints of living with his dominant elder sister Elizabeth. He had seemed destined to remain a bachelor but after his sister's death in 1938 he married the Romany lady seen here with him on their wedding day. She was a great comfort to him in his old age but within a dozen years he died and the lovely old Efail y Castell crumbled and was quickly pulled down. His grandfather, William the shoemaker, moved there in about 1840. When Joshua was a young man there was nothing to obscure the view from his front gate to Castell y Mynach and, as a postman, few houses to deliver mail to – they were mostly farms scattered over a wide area. The passing of 'Josh' and his thatched house ended an era.

Tom Jenkins ('Twm Crydd'), 1950. Twm was born on 12 June 1872 into one of the oldest Pentyrch families. His forebears had been cryddion (cobblers) in the parish for centuries. He had worked in many jobs above and below the ground during his long life but in his later years his devotion to country pursuits earned him the affectionate name 'Tom the Poacher'. His elusiveness and his noted shooting skills were so greatly admired by Colonel Henry Lewis that the landowner presented him with a pair of ornately decorated sporting guns. Several hours of tape recordings (in Welsh and English) survive of Twm recounting his life.

John Thomas, choirmaster, 1918. Under his baton, the Pentyrch Choral Society put on several memorable performances of cantatas, notably Moabites and Joseph. Singers were drawn mainly from Pentyrch but also Gwaelod y Garth, Creigiau and Taff's Well. The conductor's wife Mrs Naomi Thomas kept the choristers in tiptop vocal condition by administering Friar's Balsam at the slightest sign of a throat tickle! John ('Siôn y Cwar') was a deacon at Penuel and subsequently at Horeb.

Richard Llewellyn ('Dic Soar') and son Gwilym Trefor, with 'Caradog' at Maesteg farm, 1906. Like many Pentyrch natives, Dic was a skilful horse handler and was much in demand at parish farms. He finished his working days as the chief haulier at Nantgarw colliery. A colourful character, he lives on in verses such as the one which refers to his lack of success in wooing a local girl.

> Y deryn du pig felan, a aed di drostoi am dal?
> Oddi yma i Graig Gwilym a dishgyn ar y wal
> A gwêd wrth Mari Israel am bido bod mor ffôl
> A charu mab y ffirad… a gadael Dic ar ôl!

Joseph Frazer (1861-1940). Belfast-born Joe Frazer came to Cardiff in 1879 and quickly became well known as a local business man. As a director of Frazer and Co. Shipping Furnishers he set his staff a fine example by always being at his office before 8.00 am. He lived at Tregarth, a large house near the golf club in Creigiau, where he was regarded as the unofficial 'squire'. He contributed much to the community and was generous in his support of St Catwg's, Pentyrch and St David's in Groes Faen. His regular visits to Gwaelod y Garth where he distributed pennies are still remembered fondly by those who were village children in the 1920s and '30s.

Tregarth House, Creigiau, 1949. It was fitting that Tregarth was built by the local firm of Owen and Davies for they had indeed constructed most of the new houses in Creigiau. David Owen had already built Brynteg and Bwlchgwyn before, in partnership with his son-in-law Thomas Davies, he built the church hall as well as the houses on Llantwit Road, Cardiff Road and Pantygored Road. Tregarth was raised by Mr Davies after the passing of Mr Owen in 1919. During the time of Mr Joseph Frazer's residence there the grounds were often used for fêtes and gymkhanas.

Craig y Parc, 1950. Known locally as 'The Mansion', Craig y Parc was built during the First World War in the Lutyens English Tudor manor-house style for Thomas Evans ('Twm Glô Mân' – Tom Small Coal). The architect, who also designed the gardens, was Charles Mallows. Most of the stone used was quarried on site but dressed blocks came from Pontypridd and the colour of some features of the building suggests a Cotswolds origin. After the nationalisation of the coal industry in 1947, the mansion came under the control of the NCB. In 1955 it became a children's school run by the Spastics Society and continues as such under the auspices of SCOPE.

'Twm Glô Mân' – Thomas Evans CBE of Craig y Parc mansion in Pentyrch, the managing director of the Ocean Coal Company and director of the Barry Railway. He was a prominent figure in all docks affairs and received the CBE for his services as chairman of the committee of coal owners who acted with the Admiralty during the First World War. Mr Evans would part with a small portion of his ostentatious wealth at carol singing time when the annual tinkling of coins attracted village children like a magnet to Craig y Parc. The first singers to perform at the door would be handed a half crown from a silver tray by Davy the butler; the second group a shilling. The heap of gleaming sixpences which remained, induced some youngsters with thespian talents to don disguises and return for more.

The grandson of 'Shôn o'r Lan', John Phillips (1873-1953) was born into a family well established in the cultural and religious activities of the district. In 1901, he married Ann Watkins of Tynewydd, sister of the first chairman of the Pentyrch Parish Council and served the area for many years through the medium of local government. He became the chairman of Cardiff Rural District Council in 1920, and it was during his term of office that the footbridge over the Taff was opened and bore his name: Pont Shôn Phillip. He was both the secretary and a deacon of Capel Bethlehem, and was also a governor of the school at Gwaelod y Garth and of Howells' School, Llandaff, and later was appointed as a magistrate. A staunch supporter of all village activities, John Phillips was prominent in both the foundation, and activities of the drama groups in Gwaelod y Garth, and in an eisteddfod at Treorchy in 1920 he won an individual gold medal for his performance.

Thomas John Kemp (1895-1965), born in Gwaelod y Garth, made a considerable contribution to the life of the village. A railwayman for most of his working life, following a period in the coal industry and an active member of the Labour Party, he represented the village on the Pentyrch Parish Council for over twenty years and he was 'Father of the Council' on his retirement in 1964. An extremely active man, he was best known for his musical talents, for many years he was conductor of the Gwaelod y Garth Rechabites Childrens' Choir which performed at venues throughout South Wales, in recognition of which he was presented with a magnificent silver and ebony baton. A lifelong member of the Independent Order of the Rechabites, he organised the village Band of Hope, was a deacon of Bethlehem chapel, also secretary of the Gymanfa Ganu singing festival. He was a member of the Garth Gleemen, was closely involved in the running of the Garth Cricket Club and latterly became Chairman of the Village Hall Committee.

William James George (1904-1988). 'Bill' George was born in Fishguard, but at an early age the family moved to Maerdy where, aged thirteen, Bill began work in the colliery, being the sole breadwinner following the death of his father but left the industry after twelve years to follow a career in insurance. This led to his settling in Gwaelod y Garth where his love of music led him to become involved in the formation and activities of several choirs, the most well-known of which was the 'Garth Gleemen'. His earlier experiences in the coal industry dominated his political attitudes and in 1951 was short listed as Parliamentary Labour candidate for the local constituency. He served as a Labour councillor at both Parish and District level for many years, becoming the chairman of the Parish Council in 1960-61, but was best remembered as the Clerk to the Parish council for twenty-four years. He was made a Justice of the Peace in 1949, and held that office also for twenty-four years.

William Charles Thomas (1885-1977). 'Willie Charles', as he was universally known, lived all his life in Gwaelod y Garth. A devout Christian, he was both a lifelong member and a deacon of Bethlehem chapel. A coal miner from the age of twelve, he worked underground for thirty years until the closure of Nantgarw in 1927, following which he became a newsagent and latterly was the village postman until his retirement. He became prominent in both the Labour Party and the miners' union, serving the village as a Labour parish councillor for Gwaelod y Garth for many years and was also greatly involved in the Co-operative movement. He is remembered for his detailed knowledge of the history, geography and the geology of the local area and was one of the few villagers who saw both the erection and demolition of the Walnut Tree Viaduct.

National Eisteddfod, Cardiff, 1960. Mr T.W. Thomas of Greenhurst, Pentyrch, in his capacity as Chairman of the Eisteddfod Court, escorts Queen Elizabeth II on the day of the royal visit.

Pentyrch collectors for Cardiff Institute for the Blind, 1932. Mrs Bessie Snead is on the right and among the group are Tilly and Muriel Rogers, Evelyn Davies, Ruth and Ceridwen Llewellyn, Gladys Griffiths, Joan Morgan, Betty Evans and the Hall sisters.

John Thomas BEM (1920-1992). Born in Cardiff, John Thomas became a joiner on leaving school and served for several years in the Merchant Navy, before marrying Joan Lloyd a niece of John Foster Lloyd, Gwaelod y Garth. During their early married life in London, John won a silver medal in the Model Engineering Exhibition in 1950 for a beautiful set of $\frac{1}{8}$th scale miniature tools, all utilised in the building of a house. It was this miniaturisation which indirectly led to John's decision, following his move to Gwaelod y Garth in 1951, to devote his life to the design and manufacture of harps, a skill which had not existed in Wales for sixty years. He established a workshop and a reputation at Pear Tree Cottage, but had to cope with a disaster in 1966 when fire destroyed his workshop. Undaunted, he carried on and succeeded in passing on his skills to three other craftsmen following his move to West Wales. His reputation was acknowledged by the award of the BEM for 'Services to Craft in Wales and to Harp Making in particular'. He is pictured here with a chromatic harp which he designed and built.

Revd R.G. Berry. Robert Griffith Berry was born in Llanrwst in 1869, studied at Bangor College in North Wales, entered the ministry and was ordained as minister in Capel Bethlehem, Gwaelod y Garth in 1897. In 1903 he married Hannah Maria Watkins of Tŷ Newydd – daughter of Evan Watkins, the former manager of the Pentyrch Furnace. R.G. Berry became one of Wales' most highly respected playwrights and set up drama groups in the village, thus contributing immensely to its cultural life for young and old alike. His plays included *Asgre Lan, Noson y Farrug*, and *Yr Hen Anian*, and were regularly performed in the vestry of Capel Bethlehem. An accomplished cricketer, he played a prominent part in the establishment of the Garth Cricket Club. News of his death in 1945 caused great sorrow in the village.

Elias Atkins outside Maesarail, Gwaelod y Garth. This cottage was located in the middle of Coed Rhiw Ceiliog, and is one of the oldest in the village. Occupied at one time by Richard Jenkins, agent to the Garth iron-ore mine, the house sat astride the outcrop of a coal seam, a fact exploited to the full by one of its later inhabitants! 'Li' Atkins was the village pig slaughter man and it was said that he could complete the task including the clean-up in an hour. This activity was invariably followed by a communal 'wine tasting'.

The Gwaelod y Garth ladies WI Birthday Dinner. This one was held in the vestry of Bethlehem chapel in the mid-1950s. The branch was formed in 1952 and still meets on a regular basis, although sadly, few of the ladies pictured above are still alive.

The Gwaelod y Garth post office in 1906. The postmistress, Mary Lloyd, is standing in the doorway on the right. The two children in the foreground are Mrs Eunice Davies, and her elder brother Mr Alun Phillips. The post office and store were in the ownership of the Lloyd family from 1881 until after the Second World War.

Milk lady at Gwaelod y Garth in the 1950s. The sound of 'Anne Edwards the Milk' wheeling her cart through the village was a daily occurrence for many years, as she would carefully ladle out milk to the waiting villagers. She obtained her supply fresh from the Gedrys farm, just outside the village, where she was born, and could be relied upon whatever the weather. She later kept a small shop at No. 3 Vine Cottages, selling sweets.

Dai Evans of Cefn Colstyn was born in 1816 and became a well-known character in the farming community of Pentyrch. He died in 1900 and was survived by his favourite horse, Prince, which itself gained some fame from the posthumous bequest of its head for use in the Mari Lwyd custom! Twm and Shoni (Caerwal) 'acquired' the skull and took it on their jaunts for nearly half a century. Prince 'lives on' at the St Fagans Museum of Welsh Life where the bedecked Mari Lwyd head is on permanent display.

The Davies brothers Twm and Shoni (Caerwal) with the Mari Lwyd, 1926. They continued to use the horse's head procured from Cefn Colstyn and were the leading local exponents of the custom until the 1940s when they bequeathed Mari to the museum. At Christmas time and the New Year, the Mari Lwyd party's visits to houses and taverns were always eagerly anticipated. The clever verbal battles of wits are still remembered.

William Llewellyn, 1872. This versatile farmer of Penygarn found the time to build over a dozen houses in Pentyrch whilst running his butchery at home and a meat stall in Cardiff Market. During the 1850s he enlarged the house and outbuildings at the farm and erected the eight dwellings of nearby Penygarn Row. At the same time he served on the committee which brought about the rebuilding of St Catwg's where he was a church warden for several years. He was born in Pentyrch in 1824 and died at Penygarn in 1900.

Thomas Lee Llewellyn ('Twm Lee') born in 1875, was a notable mountain fighter and a formidable rugby forward. Known to be a gentleman on the field with an innate sense of fair play, he nevertheless had an uncommon thirst which often landed him in trouble especially during forays into Cardiff's tough dockland. A local 'hero' he was still boxing at 36 and scored memorable victories over the mighty 'Tiger' Smith. In 1917, when he was 42 years old, Twm lost one of his legs at the battle for the 'Towers of Helloc'. After the war, with his drinking now restricted to lemonade, he married the lady who had nursed him at the military hospital and they went to live beyond the Malvern Hills where he became a jobbing builder.

A gathering of the Glamorganshire Royal Observer Corps 1944. The Pentyrch branch was particularly important because the village's elevated position provided uninterrupted views of the Vale and the coast. Especially in the pre-radar days of the war, there was great dependence on the wide range of knowledge of this enthusiastic civilian force. Their operations room was well-equipped with binoculars and a large selection of up-to-date photographs of German warplanes taken from every angle. Members were expert in the identification of aircraft in flight and their instant judgement could prove crucial in the rapid mounting of defences. Enemy bombers would sometimes choose an approach route through the mist which often hung over the Bristol Channel. Once they emerged they could be detected, identified and reported extremely quickly. The look-out post on the Mountain Road was manned twenty-four hours a day and those on duty were in immediate contact with the air observation control centre in Cardiff. They could also link up with a network of airfields over south-western Britain and numerous establishments similar to their own. In this group are several Pentyrch parish men including: Fred Griffiths, Whitney Davies, Cadwgan Jones, Ithel James, David Evans, Frank Taylor, Evan Rees, Tom Clark, 'Billo' Davies, Ken Gibbon, John Rogers, 'Bob' Tanner, Stanley Moore and David Williams.

Seven

Tempus Fugit

As the lifetime of the art of photography is just a blink of an eye-lid in the span of history our record here is essentially limited. We can though rejoice in the fact that we have so many images of long disappeared places and of personages sadly departed but not forgotten. Also we cherish the photographs which recorded brief but momentous occurrences such as the sudden and mischievous trick played by the weather in the dark days of 1940 seen below. We close our collection with a few more pictures of the changing landscape and some of our timeless treasures.

Looking towards High Corner and Mountain Road from Horeb, 27 January 1940. Four months into the war, a freak ice storm hit Britain and everything came to a standstill when falling rain suddenly froze. It was as bad in Pentyrch as anywhere; dozens of trees fell under the weight of the ice and telegraph and power cables sagged to the ground. Ice-clad branches and twigs were transformed into crystal chandeliers which made music as they touched and tinkled in the gentle breeze that arose. Every minute or so a loud crack like the sound of gunfire could be heard as yet another tree surrendered. No freezing rainstorm of such severity has occurred since.

Pentyrch - from the Garth.

View from The Warren, 1934. This shows the flat part of the mountain road known as 'the Dwattan' or alternatively 'Gwattan', which is effectively the watershed whence streams flow eastwards to the Taff and westwards to the Ely river. Still visible at this time were the ruins of Gelynog called the 'Three Chimneys', long the home of the Jenkins family (the Cryddion) shoemakers, not just cobblers. In 1841 two members of the Jenkins family and three apprentices/journeymen worked in this little shoe factory. Also visible are the white-washed Horeb, Penuel and the old Wesleyan meeting rooms at the bottom of Temperance Row. In this early September scene, George Llewellyn has a full barn of hay at Blaenbielli.

Cave in Lesser Garth, 1951. The natural cave network of the Lesser Garth hill managed miraculously to escape the effects of extensive iron-ore mining and massive limestone quarrying close by. It was here in the natural caverns and passages that Stone Age axe heads and various animal bones were discovered some years ago.

114

Penygarn Stores just prior to demolition, 1977. The shop run by William Evans from 1860 until his death in 1910, was more than a village store; it was a remarkable emporium stocking a huge range of goods including fifty-four varieties of cigars, seventy kinds of biscuits and cake; candles and lampblack, oil, soap, wines, whisky and brandy, horse and cattle food, fruit and vegetables, furniture, drapery and hosiery, salted meats, tools and implements, buttons and gunpowder! He insisted on his staff speaking the native tongue (for the populace was monoglot Welsh) and preferred them to be Calvinistic Methodist like himself: he was the senior deacon at Horeb chapel (opposite the shop).

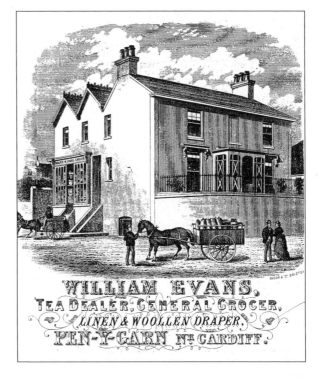

Lower Mountain Road, 1949, looking towards High Corner. The garden hedge of Ty'nywaun is on the left and in the centre, Cambria Terrace. Out of picture on the right is where the Scout Hut (formerly known as the 'Rest Centre') is located.

Cambria Terrace, Mountain Road, 1949. One of three blocks of houses built in the 1850s to meet the increased demand for accommodation for the families of ironworkers and miners, it was demolished in 1955. The barking of Twm the Poacher's spaniels and terriers coming from the tin shack on the right was a familiar sound in the 1930s. Today the council houses of Penycwm stand on the site.

Ty'nywaun Row, 1938. This was a terrace of six sturdy houses demolished along with many others in Penygarn during 1955. They had no back entrances, no sanitation, and water had to be carried in the traditional way. It is now thought, however, that they could have been converted with a little ingenuity into desirable residences.

Penygarn Row, just before demolition in the early 1960s. Like many other dwellings in Pentyrch, domestic amenities were poor. On the right can be seen the entrance to the communal open-air tap house from which all the householders had to carry their water, whatever the weather.

Built about 1848 but now an overgrown ruin, 'The Bowers' (aptly named) was home to many before it was evacuated in 1947, when the families who lived on the side of the Garth Hill were rehoused on the Garth Newydd estate. Not all of the families, however, were happy with the move, as many did not have the opportunity to continue to enhance their income by keeping pigs and chickens, amongst the restrictions of living on a modern estate.

Ivy Cottage, on the side of the Garth Hill, displays the trademark of the occupant Harley Welsby who always built a dovecote at his home. His wife and son are also in the picture. Most of the cottages on Garth Hill were built between 1840 and 1860, during a period of rapid expansion in the area, to accommodate the manpower requirements of the mining industry. The many sandstone quarries high on the Garth provided the raw material for the buildings.

Caerwen (White Fortress), 1965. This nineteenth-century farmhouse on the south face of the Garth is now a complete ruin. The name is a puzzle to some, but the local oral tradition holds that a thousand years ago there was a small fort here which acted as a look-out down to the coastal regions where the Vikings had settlements. Archaeologists have failed to find it, but they have just not looked hard enough! A respected scholar suggests 'Cae'r Ywen' might have been its original name, which seems a nice idea. 'Rubbish,' say the traditionalists, there is no yew tree in miles!

Although the amenities of the cottages on the Garth Hill were not in accordance with the demands of modern society, the views were nevertheless magnificent. This view is from the rear of Bower House looking over Ivy Cottages to the valley floor beyond.

Prior to the opening of the footbridge in 1926, the only means of crossing the river at the top end of the village was by ferry. Here the water was very deep due to the construction of the weir, and several lives were lost to the Taff over the years, including that of the wife of the ferryman. Although seemingly tranquil, the river was capable of violent flooding, making the ferry crossing inoperable and isolating Taff's Well from Gwaelod y Garth.

The construction of the footbridge in 1925/26. The bridge, Pont Shôn Phillip, was opened by John Phillips JP in 1926, and replaced the ferry which had operated for a hundred years. The Taff was a notoriously dangerous river, and Leland writing in the 1530s, noted that all of the bridges were then made of timber, 'The waters of Taphe cummith so down from woddy hilles and often bringgith down such logs and trees, that the countery wer not able to make up the bridges if they were stone they should be so often broken.'

Capel House, Llanilterne, 1895. A fine old farmhouse below Capel church, it was for many years the village inn where the Williams family of Parc, the local justices, held the Petty Sessions in the eighteenth century. In the early nineteenth century their successors the Lewises promoted the hunt suppers there. The licence was transferred to The Star shortly before 1851.

Efail y Castell, 1920. Originally the castle smithy, the two cottages, together with the rare, thatched, round pig sty, were demolished in the early 1950s and replaced by a children's playground. The left-hand cottage was occupied for many years by the Jenkins family. Edwin Jenkins was a shoemaker and postmaster. His sister Miss Elizabeth Jenkins succeeded him in the post office. Within the memory of older villagers, Miss Jenkins was a formidable lady, presiding sternly over her stock of sweets, cough medicines and syrup of figs. Her strong opposition to the 'Demon Drink' kept the Creigiau Hotel, across the road, a temperance establishment for many years.

The Mathew Tew Bench. One of the seventeenth-century Mathews remembered as Mathew Tew (Fat Mathew), had a reputation as a bullying squire. He boasted that his golden guineas, laid side by side, would stretch from Castell y Mynach to Pentyrch church. One of several versions of a local legend is that he was done to death in Efail y Castell by a cottager who placed a shoemaker's awl under a cushion on a bench upon which the squire habitually sat! The bench was preserved in Castell y Mynach until a few years ago.

Old Village looking southwards, 1936. The first dwelling on the left is Tŷ Ffald.

Tŷ Rhawn, Old Village, 1908. The gentleman in the doorway is Daniel Thomas who kept the Rock and Castle pub for nearly forty years.

Creigiau farm, *c.* 1900, viewed from Craig Ffynnon Dwym, the suggested site of Criga Castle. On the right Cefn Gwarwig can just be seen and above it, to the left, the buildings of Llwynybrain. The clump of trees towards the upper left mark the position of a former farmstead called Tir William Harry, probably the same as that called Cefn Gwarwig Isaf. It ceased to be occupied in the eighteenth-century and is represented at present by a ruined barn.

Creigiau station, *c.* 1910. The Barry railway built by David Davies of Llandinam was completed in July 1889 to carry coal from Trehafod to Davies's new Barry Dock. By 1896 it was opened to passenger traffic and a station erected on part of a farm known as Criga. Deciding that Creigiau was the correct spelling the company so named the new landmark. From this beginning the village has evolved.

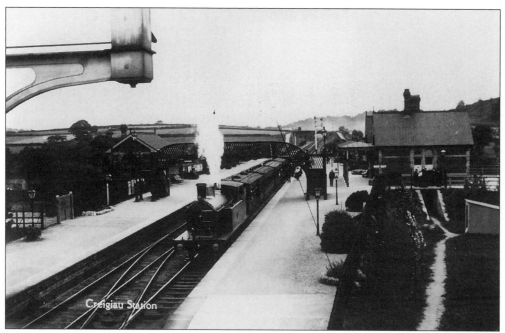

Creigiau *c.* 1920. The station which helped to put Creigiau on the map was used by colliers of Pentyrch going to work in the valley mines, businessmen commuting to Cardiff and families on trips to Barry Island. It became known for its well-kept appearance with its regularly brushed platforms, scrubbed benches and pretty flower beds.

Creigiau *c.* 1920. The beginnings of the village as viewed from the field overlooking Mr Perrett's market garden; he had not yet built the greenhouse. The station appears on the right and the Barry cottages on the left. Behind we see the Creigiau Hotel and Station Terrace; the upper Terrace had also been completed. Just visible in the background, behind the station, is Creigiau Villa which had replaced the old cottage known as 'Ty'r Ysgol'.

Temperance Road, 1890. No doubt the residents of this street were of admirably sober habits. There was no public house here but there was a Wesleyan meeting house, a post office, a bakehouse renowned locally for its bread and there was also a police lock-up. The latter would have been conveniently placed with regard to the occasional attempt by someone to disprove the appropriateness of the street's name! It was the busiest thoroughfare in the village so perhaps this was a Sunday.

View from Horeb Corner, 1907, with one of William Evans's delivery carts returning to the store. Children play around the shop steps, an activity that continued for another sixty years. In the centre beyond the telegraph pole the thatched roof of High Corner cottage can just be seen.

This cromlech, a megalithic tomb, has stood at Caeryrfa for five thousand years and is a listed ancient monument.

The 'Pimple' on the Garth is a 4,000-year-old burial mound dating from the Middle Bronze Age and was NOT, as one modern legend claims, raised to bring the hill to a thousand feet above sea level. It is one of a small number of tumuli on the mountain from the same period which are protected by strict laws relating to the preservation of listed ancient monuments. Its position on the northern skyline makes it the most prominent prehistoric landmark in the district.

Acknowledgements

Pentyrch and District Local History Society gratefully acknowledges the help it received from numerous people during the preparation of this book. In particular, we wish to thank those who readily supplied the photographs for publication and those who worked so assiduously in collecting them. If there are any omissions, we would be pleased to make copies of any appropriate pictures which slipped through the net, for our records. We credit with thanks: Mrs Ann Beech (pp. 49, 81b, 104a); Mrs A. Betty (p. 29b); Arthur Boobier (p. 67b); Mrs Nancy Castle (pp. 46, 85a, 89a, 95a-left, 108b); Lady Connor (p. 64b); Selwyn Cook (p. 95 a-right); Mrs R. Cugley (pp. 10b, 11a); Mrs Audrey Davies (pp. 12a, 114a); Barry Davies (pp. 42a, 79b, 83b, 87b, 88a, 98, 99); Ellis Davies (p. 95b-right); Mrs Winnie Davies (p. 36); Mrs Peggy Davies (pp. 90, 96a); Billy Evans (pp. 95a, 110a); Clay Evans (p. 109a); Glyn Evans (p. 39a); Illtyd Evans (p. 95b-left); Graham George (p. 105a); Mrs Margaret Griffiths (p. 112a); Mrs Rene Griffiths (p. 80b); Miss E. Jenkins (p. 100a); Mrs R. Jenkins (p. 121); Roger John (p. 20); Mrs Jan Johnson (pp. 27b, 43b); Mrs Val Johnson (pp. 38b, 101a); Henry Jones (p. 80a); Mrs Ruth Jones (pp. 17b, 106b); Brian Joyce (pp. 29a, 53b, 123b); Eifion Kemp (pp. 55, 104b); Alwyn Lindsey (pp. 21a, 22a, 26, 27a, 28b, 85b); Miss Barbara Llewellyn (p. 67a); Mrs Diana Llewellyn (p.78b); Don Llewellyn (pp. 6, 8, 13, 14, 15, 16, 17a, 18, 21b, 25a, 28a, 30b, 31, 32, 34, 37, 38a, 39b, 40, 47, 48, 53a, 56a, 57a, 58, 61, 62a, 65, 66a, 70b, 71, 72b, 73, 74, 75, 76, 78a, 79a, 82a, 83a, 86, 87a, 88b, 89b, 91a, 92a, 94, 96b, 97b, 100b, 102a, 103, 105b, 108a, 110b, 111b, 114b, 115, 116, 117, 119a, 120, 123a, 126, 127); Miss Kitty Llewellyn (pp. 42b, 68a, 111a); Raymond Llewellyn (pp. 12b, 81a); Tom Llewellyn (p. 92b); Alan Lock (p. 68b); Mrs Shirley Lyons (p. 77); Mrs Joan Miles (p. 45a); Dafydd Millward (pp. 41, 43a, 44); Denis Murphy (p. 113); Pentyrch Community Council (pp. 33a, 52a, 54, 56b, 57a, 62b, 64a, 70a, 72a, 82a, 84, 102b, 122a, 124, 125); Mrs Doris Pulfrey (pp. 50b, 66b); Haydn Pulfrey (pp. 45b, 50a, 91b); Mrs Olive Reed (p. 2); Mrs Lena Richards (p. 107b); Russell Seale (p. 69); Mrs J H Southcliffe (p. 24); Graham Stevens (p. 51b); Mrs Pat Stone (p. 109b); Derek Thomas (p. 33b); Mrs Joan Thomas (p. 107a); T.W. Thomas (pp. 101b, 106a); Arthur Welsby (pp. 23b, 25b, 51a, 118, 119b); Mrs Margery Wibley (p. 23a); Mrs Eryl Williams (pp. 30a, 52b, 63, 93); Gerwyn Williams (p. 60); Mrs E.Whitticombe (pp. 10a, 11b, 22b).

Letters 'a' (above) and 'b' (below) indicate the position of the photographs on each page.

This book was compiled by Ellis Davies and Don Llewellyn with considerable help from Barry Davies, Derek Thomas, Tom Llewellyn and Arthur Llewellyn. The society also wishes to record its indebtedness to Simon Eckley of the Chalford Publishing Company for his valuable help and guidance.

Anyone wishing to become a member of Pentyrch and District Local History Society should contact: the secretary, Mrs Megan Rogers, 29 Bronllwyn, Pentyrch or the treasurer, Mrs Liz Wallek, Tŷ Rhawn, Old Village, Pentyrch.